Campervan Capers

A Couple's First Year
Exploring the World of Campervanning

Alannah Foley

Copyright © 2012 Alannah Foley
All rights reserved.

No part of this publication may be reproduced, stored in a retrieval system,
or transmitted, in any form or by any means, graphic, electronic,
mechanical, photocopying, recording or otherwise,
without the prior permission of the author.
Thank you for respecting the hard work of this author.

ISBN-13: 978-1478271949

CONTENTS

	PREFACE (PRE-RAMBLE)	i
	INTRODUCTION	iii
1	**Maiden Voyage** September – Devon – Newton Abbot area	1
2	**The Undiscovered Doorstep** September – West Cornwall	7
3	**Stretching our Wheels** October – Somerset (en route to Wales)	15
4	**The Welsh Leek Conspiracy** October – Wales and return via Bristol	20
5	**Damp Squibs & Snowy Rooftops** Dealing with the inevitability of winter	32
6	**Out of Hibernation** Here comes the spring sunshine… Making new plans	36
7	**Dawdling Round Dorset** April – Dorset	39
8	**Peak Experiences** May – Peak District, Derbyshire	46
9	**Journey to the Past** May – Return from Derbyshire via Staffordshire	63
10	**Star-Struck** June – Devon	72

11	**The Magic of Cornwall** July – Cornwall	84
12	**Dipping into Devon** August – Devon	86
13	**Modern Wheels & Ancient Stones** September – Somerset (incl Motorhome Show) and Wiltshire	95
	EPILOGUE – The End of the Road?	113
	30 TOP TIPS for the Novice	115
	CONSIDERATIONS WHEN BUYING A Motorhome or Caravan	118
	USEFUL WEBLINKS for each Chapter	121
	FAUX REVIEWS by Pseudo-Celebrities for Campervan Capers	130
	ABOUT the Author	132
	CONNECT with the Author	133
	OTHER TITLES by the Author	134

PREFACE (PRE-RAMBLE)

Oh, goodie! A preface! I really love writers wittering on, when all I want to do is get on and read the story!

(Don't worry, this one is only short and has headings for easy reading...)

"DISCLAIMERS"

Reader Discernment
I haven't included anything in the book which I believe to be inaccurate or 'shonky'. Still, readers will all be different and have varying needs, so use your own discernment in interpreting my experiences, checking out links and taking on advice. What's right for us may not be right for you.

Opinions on each site are my own and others may have a different viewpoint. I have also endeavoured to ensure information is correct as far as possible, but make no guarantee that my facts are beyond reproach. I cannot take responsibility for anyone else's experience of a site or the fact that information may have changed since our travels.

Caravan Club
Part-way through the book, we joined the Caravan Club. I would emphasise that we are not representatives of the Caravan Club. The aim of our membership was to trial it and see what we thought. I have endeavoured to report as objectively as possible – as I have done with all other sites – so that readers might benefit from our experiences.

Although I have mentioned some of the Caravan Club's 'CL' sites by name (with the Club's permission), be reminded that they are exclusive to Club members and full listings are given in the Club directory which you receive upon joining. For information on the Caravan Club, visit www.caravanclub.co.uk.

Current Information
Any site fees are mentioned for reasons of comparison only and were current in the period covered by the book (2009/2010). However,

whilst prices quickly go out of date, information and tips will still be relevant and useful for the most part.

All chapter links (at the end of the book) were active and correct at completion of the book's manuscript and I don't endorse one company, organisation or website over another.

INTRODUCTION

A Brief Overview...
This book tells the story of a couple's first year in their first-ever campervan. That couple is me and my partner, Steve. And in the book, I seek to blend flowing travel tale with humour and insight, whilst sharing some of the more earthy practical aspects.

Who is the Book for?
The main audience I had in mind when writing the book was those who own a campervan/motorhome or caravan, or dream of doing so. Our mini adventures may also appeal to travel enthusiasts in general.

Whilst I do not claim to be an expert, I hope the novice (or would-be) will benefit from the practical tips we've picked up along the way (several are summarised in the section "30 Top Tips for the Novice" at the end of the book for easy reference.)

As our travels all took place within Great Britain (see Contents for details), non-UK residents considering a campervan or caravan holiday here may also find the book useful. Therefore, I've attempted to consider an international audience with little knowledge of the country, its seasons or its holiday periods.

Other Considerations
Throughout the book, I've endeavoured to consider a range of vehicles and owners, yet the world of motorhoming is so vast, it would be impossible to cover everything or everyone. Similarly, as this story is about me and my partner – a childless couple in our forties who have only ever owned a Transit-sized camper – this inevitable bias will no doubt come through.

At the time of writing, people are watching their purse strings a lot more than they used to. I have therefore sought to emphasise holidaying on a budget – no doubt leaving you to wonder who is the biggest cheapskate – us, or the reader?

The original manuscript for this book was created for digital publication. Therefore, I've made a few minor changes when subsequently adapting it for print.

Photographs
An online collection of our travel photos can be found at:: www.flickr.com/photos/alannah_foley/sets, along with a map showing an overview of trips at:: www.flickr.com/photos/alannah_foley/7102090827.

And there's more...
At the end of the book, you'll find a summary of practical tips, reference links for each chapter, and links to the Campervan Capers blog, my website and information on my other works.

Anyway, enough of that!

Now kick back with a cuppa and **enjoy the book...**

Alannah Foley
Cornwall, England
April 2012

~ 1 ~
MAIDEN VOYAGE

Blue skies and sunshine were companions that could only inspire optimism as we eagerly headed up the highway in our 'new' second-hand campervan. An invitation to a family barbecue in Newton Abbot, south Devon, was all the excuse my partner Steve and I needed to plan a long weekend away.

Our trip might only be a humble local jaunt, but we hoped it would be the first in a long line of journeys planned to keep my itchy feet at bay. You see, in my twenties, I'd always had what some might call a restless spirit, never staying anywhere for too long. But after meeting Steve in my mid-thirties, I finally got a taste of what it was like to 'settle down'.

Whilst this state of affairs had many redeeming qualities, I soon hit my forties and – hey presto! – a mid-life crisis! Or at least, that's what I told myself it was. Either way, neither of us had the travel bug badly enough to warrant uprooting our lives completely. Yet I, for one, definitely needed a bit of adventure… And then the campervan came along.

In August 2009, we chanced upon an old Autosleeper Flair at a bargain price, and over a weekend, we decided to buy it, thinking it would be a great compromise for our situation. Now we could up-sticks whenever we felt the need, yet still keep our home lives going. We could at least experiment for a year, couldn't we? Then if it wasn't for us, we could always try something else.

So here we were, on our first-ever trip in our first-ever campervan. And, after only a few hours' drive from our home in Cornwall, getting lofty views over the hedges that we'd never seen from the car, we pulled in at our campsite, enthusiastic about putting our new four-wheeled acquisition to the test.

The Twelve Oaks Farm caravan site was a peaceful working farm that had been 'upgraded' to make way for holidaymakers. We'd found out about it from an old holiday parks guide left inside the 'van, and booked easily by email; and it was only a short drive from Steve's cousin's house, where the Sunday barbecue was being held.

Now into September, the main British holiday season was over and there were plenty of spare pitches to choose from. We selected a spot on a slight incline and rooted round in the 'van, pulling out what looked like thin wedges of bright yellow cheese fit for a giant's lunch box: these were the 'van levellers; and, propped under the front wheels, it was hoped they would stop us from gradually sliding down the bed during the night.

For this, our maiden voyage into the Great Unknown, we'd done little planning, and we knew sweet Fanny Adams about campervans. So, with no manual for the 'van, it looked like we'd have to wing things for a while. The table support poles, for example, were niftily housed in a 'pocket' above the side door. Luckily, Steve being taller than me, he could see them. We also hadn't booked a pitch with electric hookup and, before leaving, had discovered the leisure battery was flat, so we'd have to use lamps and torches once it got dark.

After an easy-cook meal, I popped out to wash the dishes, leaving Steve to set up the bed. Although our 'van had a sink, better to use the site's more spacious washing-up facilities instead. Relaxing at the sink, I revelled in the sheer simplicity of having only a single bowl of washing-up in front of me. It certainly seemed much more minimalistic than our usual after-meal sprawl in the kitchen at home. *What a simple life this campervanning is,* I thought. I probably hadn't enjoyed doing the dishes this much in years.

The blessed silence was broken by a chap clattering a large pile of washing-up onto the drainer beside me. As we chatted, it turned out that he still had two more loads yet to come, as he and his wife had had a roast dinner that night. *Crikey!* We didn't even have an oven in our 'van, let alone four hobs to cook on. Yet, despite my love of a roast, I didn't relish the thought of making one in our little 'van. Surely it'd be easier to eat out at the pub instead? I stood there, basking in our apparent relative poverty whilst the poor bloke continued to bemoan his mountain of evening-time chores.

Back at the 'van, Steve was still setting up the bed. Now, it turns out that some 'vans have fixed beds and some have what are called rock-and-roll beds (one tug and the backseat converts to a flat bed). Unfortunately, ours was more like a Krypton Factor-style jigsaw puzzle in comparison, so we wanted to set it up before dark rather than leave ourselves fumbling about by the half-light of our torches trying to piece it together.

Technically, it was possible to have a transverse bed in our Transit-sized camper (a much quicker setup), but since Steve was too tall to sleep across the width of the 'van, we had to fold down the front seats and make up the bed using every bit of 'furniture' instead. The good thing about our setup at least, was that the kitchen area was still accessible. With a rock-and-roll bed, certain cupboards would be off-limits.

As we finished piecing the bed together, we began to feel a bit like sardines in our 'tin can' 'van, with every bit of space gradually being filled with seat blocks, blankets and enough pillows to stuff a giant toy whale. As forty-somethings, we were still agile enough to fiddle with such bed setups, but wait another decade or two and we might not want to risk pulling a muscle or ratchetting our spines out of joint.

My first night's sleep wasn't exactly blissful comfort. But then, we hadn't thought to 'test drive' the bed beforehand either. If you've ever come across the old fairy tale about the Princess and the Pea, then you'll get the picture of how annoyingly sensitive I am when it comes to feeling every bump and cushion-join underneath me. However, wriggling about, I managed to find the comfy spots, and finally got some sleep.

The next morning, we peered gingerly out through the curtains to see occasional bods walking across the site lawns in dressing-gowns and pyjamas. Watching the holidaymakers make their way to the shower block uninhibited, I thought the scene might not look out of place in a convalescent home or a lunatic asylum (oops! – sorry! – political correctness alert! – I meant to say 'wellness recovery centre'). Other folk walked back and forth pulling what looked like an old-fashioned roller-type lawn-mower. It was a nifty, cylindrical container with a long handle that rolled along (called an 'aqua-roll') and saved you carrying a heavy weight of water from tap to motorhome.

Later, we visited Steve's cousin Lisa and her partner Simon, and they kindly offered to show us around the area, suggesting we went for a walk on Dartmoor, the nearby National Park which is well known for its wild, moorland landscapes and granite outcrops. It certainly was a lovely sunny day for it, and they'd even drive us, so we could leave the campervan parked outside their place.

Now, Simon's a lovely chap, but nobody warned me that he drives like a Frenchman. His nippy driving technique reminded me of my teen years when I was driven at high speed around tight bends by some relative or other of my French exchange partner. There was snow on the roads, yet the guy drove as if he was trying to catch Santa's sleigh on its way out of town. And, looking back now, it's hard to say whether he was drunk or stoned into the bargain (the guy, not Santa). Fortunately, in our present-day scenario, there was no snow, but the car certainly wasn't gathering any moss.

We survived the drive, parked up and I unhooked my fingernails from the car seat. Led along grassland and tracks, we eventually came to Hound Tor, a beautiful granite outcrop to the east of Dartmoor. We lay down to rest on the rocks, basking like lizards in the heat of the sun. Down below on the hillside, stones marked out the remains of an old settlement and, if Wikipedia is to be believed, this was a deserted medieval village called Hundatora, excavated between 1961 and 1975.

Simon led us to a river in the shelter of a peaceful, wooded valley and, after more walking in the beating sunshine, we eventually returned to the car and I fastened my seatbelt pending another demonstration from the Gallic Driving School Meister.

The next day was again full of bright sunshine, and we enjoyed a family barbecue at Lisa and Simon's place (the initial reason for our journey) before heading back to our site. Someone told us there was a heated swimming pool on site, but it was too late for a dip now, even if we'd remembered to bring our swimming gear.

Getting ready to leave the next day, we made use of the on-site recycling facilities then turned to see that the dreaded porta-potty loo was staring us in the face. Try as one might to avoid it, it had to be dealt with. We'd inherited it with the 'van and, thankfully, the previous owners had had the good manners to empty and clean it thoroughly before unleashing it onto a new owner.

I'd only ever come across one of these portable toilets once before: on a barge holiday when I was eighteen – although I couldn't remember anyone stopping off to empty it anywhere. Perhaps, not wanting to draw attention to it, someone had crept away to 'do the deed'? Anyway, after some consternation, we plucked up the courage to ask at reception. We let out a sigh of relief when they explained that there was a chemical disposal facility on site. Now all we had to do was work out how to empty the thing – and I wasn't sure British etiquette stretched to getting the reception staff to give us a demonstration.

Although it was clear that Steve was the only one strong enough to lift a full porta-loo without strain, we'd only been away for a couple of days (and had toilets on site), so it was light enough for me to draw the short straw for the first dastardly empty-and-cleanup session. After an initial shudder at the thought, I went to the designated area to try and solve another Krypton Factor-style jigsaw puzzle: how to take the contraption apart without spraying the contents all over myself! Luckily, the task wasn't as difficult – or as off-putting – as I'd thought it would be. I survived!

We bought some local produce from the little shop on site before leaving and drove to a nearby nature reserve (Stover Country Park) that we'd earmarked on our journey over. A large wooden information hut near the entrance was surrounded by trees; and, as we walked through, they opened out onto a lake frilled by yet more trees. The park, it turned out, covers 114 acres and is a mixture of grassland, heathland, coniferous and deciduous woodland, marshland, lakes and ponds. Not surprising, then, that on this good-weather day, there were quite a few parents milling about with their kids – the park clearly sets out to attract families, evidenced by the nature and heritage trails, picnic areas and sculptures tucked away in the surrounding forest.

After a campervan lunch, we intended to head straight home, but stumbled on a large camping outlet with caravans, motorhomes and huge tents on display outside. It was too enticing to pass by. The indoor shop area was no less grandiose, with an eye-boggling array of kit to ensure campers were kept firmly out of the Dark Ages.

We'd always thought that camping and motorhoming were about simplicity and getting back to the basics. But, far from being guided in that direction, it seemed, campers were being seductively chaperoned into recreating the comfort and convenience of their own homes with all manner of gadgets and gizmos – some essential, many not. From mini TVs to toilet facilities, from toasters to top-loading clothes washers, no expense had been spared in reinventing mod cons, usually in a more compact form. A home from home indeed!

As we headed down the highway, we reflected on our visit to the camping outlet. We might *like* the idea of whittling down our personal possessions into the small, simple space of a campervan, but with such 'sweetshops' around, how easy would it be for motor-homers to avoid temptation and go on a campervan diet?

We found no further interesting reasons to detour from our path home, and got back with plenty of time to unpack. Our first trip away was an adventure we relished, one which had been blessed by the September sunshine. We might only have stayed away for two nights, but it had whetted our appetites for more, and we couldn't wait to plan at least one other journey before the fortuitous British weather decided to shut up shop…

~ 2 ~
THE UNDISCOVERED DOORSTEP

By now, we were discovering just how well-guarded a secret motorhoming was. Before our campervan purchase, we never knew anyone who had a 'van – or, at least, we didn't *think* we did! No sooner had we spread the news of our purchase, than several friends wriggled out of the woodwork and confessed to already owning one.

"You'll *love* having a camper! It opens up a whole new world," they'd enthuse as they went on to talk about short breaks away and the sheer joy of having a convenient mini home on wheels. Inadvertently, we seemed to have joined some kind of unofficial club that was taking us under its wing.

With a motorhome or caravan, it seems you can forget the old paradigm of two standard holidays a year. We remembered watching a TV show where a couple took twelve caravan breaks away each year, rather than the one, mad-dash overseas holiday – and all within easy reach of home.

Some months back, we'd drawn up a list of local destinations which we wanted to visit some day. You know, those places close by that the tourists always visit, but locals rarely do? Since we were lucky enough to live in Cornwall – one of Britain's top holiday destinations – why not make the most of it? There were so many places on our doorstep which could easily get overlooked. And, now that we had the campervan, we could disappear for a few days instead of making the usual daytrip, and take things in at a slower pace.

We liked the idea of visiting west Cornwall, with its rugged coastline and ancient past. And, although I'd lived down that way some years back, I still hadn't managed to visit all the tourist sites.

Some of the things we enjoyed doing were visiting caves, mines and other prehistoric sites; and there was plenty to see here in that regard. West Cornwall is steeped in folklore with tales of giants having once lived in the area. Some say the legends come from the fact that 'visiting' Vikings had an average height much bigger than that of the native Cornish. There is also a high concentration of standing stones and ancient sites, as well as a whole network of mines on the west coast.

As members of this new unofficial campervanning family, we found we were getting friendly waves from motorhomes passing in the opposite direction as we travelled along the highway south. It reminded me of what an ex-boyfriend called *The Bikers' Nod:* an acknowledging nod to fellow motorbike riders who, by virtue of the fact that they rode a motorbike, were deemed to belong to a grand fraternity of bikers. It seemed that, because we had a campervan (even a lowly old Transit-sized one) we were party to what we later dubbed *The Campervanner's Wave*.

The first town we stopped off at was the small coastal town of Hayle. Although its Cornish name, Heyl, means 'estuary', the tourist blurb prefers to play up its 'three miles of golden sands' description instead. The town had supposedly been up for big development years back, although the only evidence of it so far was a 'bolt-on' shopping zone on the outskirts. In summer, Hayle and nearby St Ives are very popular, but it was now the end of September and, with kids back at school after the holidays, it was a quieter place, even now, on a Friday afternoon.

We drove on to Trencrom Hill a few miles away, hoping to park outside a friend's place for the night. However, since he was away, we decided to sleep overnight in a small car park tucked away nearby. Camping out in rural areas is what's known in the trade as 'wild camping' (aka 'boondocking' in America); and it's something I still have mixed feelings about.

Despite the fact that such off-the-beaten-track car parks seem peaceful on the surface, they can often be an attractive stomping ground for pyromaniac boy racers who want to test out the fire-retardant properties of their stolen vehicles. This might be a rare occurrence, and overnight stays in a camper which left the driver's seat accessible once the bed was set up, would leave you open for a quick-getaway should trouble arrive in your parking spot. But with our bed setup (where the front seats made up the bottom half of the bed), we didn't have that option.

If someone fancied setting fire to our tyres (a 'tyromaniac'?), they'd be melted by the time we rejigged the seats to drive off. It wasn't a positive image to have in mind, and only served to remind me that maybe I was starting to turn into my parents – thinking in a way I promised myself I never would. Even so, such fears put paid to the alter ego's romantic notions of travelling where the tide takes you and bedding up for the night in the bosom of nature.

We've often seen motorhomes parked up on the side of a main road at night and wondered why they haven't sought out a more secluded spot (perhaps due to fear of the above-mentioned 'tyromaniacs'?). Even when we've parked up for a cuppa on the side of a main road, we've been constantly buffeted by the wind. Would you even get any sleep parked up there? Or would the swaying feel like maternal rocking to some folk, helping them get a better night's kip?

Before tucking ourselves in for the evening, we walked up Trencrom, since the weather was glorious, calm and clear. On a map, the Cornish peninsula is like a cinched waist here (only about five miles across), so we had views of Hayle on the north coast and St Michael's Mount (a mini tidal island) to the south, as well as green fields and hill vistas all round.

On our last (and first!) trip away, I hadn't found our jigsaw-style bed that comfy, and in order to provide a good night's sleep, we considered all sorts of options. Was it a case of having to get the 'van reupholstered? That could be pricey. Or would we have to buy a more comfy 'van? One with a rock-and-roll bed? It seemed too early to consider such a drastic measure for something which might be rectifiable in some other way.

Fortunately, it turns out that I'm not the only 'Princess and the Pea' type around. Many other folk also find they need some kind of cushioning on top of their beds, even in a more expensive, swish 'van. A roll of memory foam is usually the order of the day, but we later spotted a couple of foam rolls in a camping shop and took the cheapskate route. They didn't take up much room and, although they weren't a perfect solution, I had a much more comfy sleep, the foam adding a modicum of softness to the firm bed blocks and smoothing out the offending joins between blocks. My Princess and the Pea syndrome might not have been totally cured, but if it ended up being a long-term gripe, I could always go the memory foam route.

Rather than breakfast in our enclosed car park the next morning, we decided to find somewhere with a view, and drove around, chancing upon a large layby. With views stretching out towards St Michael's

Mount on the south coast, the parking spot would undoubtedly have accommodated numerous motorhomes over the years. As we ate our cooked English breakfast, we noticed the name of the house opposite: Blue Horizons.

"Hmm..." mused Steve, "They should rename it 'White Campervan Views'!"

Our first destination of the day was Chysauster, an ancient village a few miles north of Penzance, run by English Heritage. Our way was barred by a cow that had made a valiant escape from a field. It was lolling about in the road, obviously overwhelmed by the choices generated by its new-found freedom. Although I admired its enterprising spirit, anarchy was sure to break out before long, with its Friesian pals following behind (like sheep?) – and then the whole road would be totally clogged up! So, with the help of an equally-delayed motorist coming from the opposite direction, the cow was finally coaxed back to Bovine HQ.

In the height of the British summer, Chysauster is apparently bustling with group tours. However, now at the start of autumn, there were no tours and we had to chaperone ourselves around. Perhaps it was a ploy to get us to buy the informative guidebook – if so, it worked a treat. To avoid disappointment, it's worth remembering that normal routines might change out of season – or that some attractions close altogether – so it's always best to check the situation before you go away.

In any case, the site had free parking, toilets and an enthusiastic site attendant with a claim to fame. Apparently, she'd appeared on TV – not only on the Weakest Link show hosted by the restrained Ann Robinson, but she had also taken part in some kind of 'shopping trolley challenge' programme presented by the effervescent Dale Winton. Had we been a bit more on the ball, we could have got our guidebook autographed by a potential celebrity. I bet we'll be kicking ourselves one day. Hindsight, eh?

Chysauster is one of several ancient sites in this part of Cornwall and here, you can still see what's left of circular dwellings set on a hillside, with distant views across the south Cornwall coast. The skies were turning overcast and the wind had started blowing; and it certainly gave me an appreciation of what it must have been like living there hundreds of years ago. Were there shelter-giving trees around the site back then? If not, it surely must have been a harsh life in the depths of winter. Just imagine an Iron Age estate agent trying to sell the place: *Nice views, but it's cold as hell!* Not exactly what you'd call 'Location, Location, Location'!

The guidebook was packed with information and enabled us to build a good picture of the layout from the remains. Being a gardener myself, I was also struck by the 'garden terraces' on the lower side of the dwellings. The whole settlement was much more sophisticated than one might have guessed.

Although this part of west Cornwall isn't exactly flat, with few patches of trees for protection, it has an openness that leaves it vulnerable to the full brunt of the elements. In response, the landscape has become rugged and tempered – with shrub-filled moors that are more wind*chiselled* rather than wind*swept*. On a blustery, overcast day, it can look atmospheric and haunting (what the locals call drab'n'dreary); and when the sun shines, colours that a dull day had bleached away suddenly radiate their beauty: purple and pink heathers, yellow gorses, or multi-coloured hedgerows, depending on the season.

Despite the 'Cathy and Heathcliff' appeal of the place, the buffeting wind eventually won us over and we retreated to Penzance to do a bit of shopping before heading out west to our site at Roseland Park near St Just.

Prior to our trip, I'd consulted our trusty yet out-of-date parks guide and surfed the internet to research sites. The good thing about checking out details on the internet is that you can select sites that reflect your needs. As a couple without kids, we weren't seeking a busy family site with entertainments laid on and didn't need a swimming pool for the kids. We were just after a no-frills, quiet break away. And once I'd found two or three sites in the area that fit the bill, I compared them for facilities, cost and the general 'vibe' based on their website (most had site photographs).

We were planning our trip at short notice, so instead of filling out a website booking form, we made enquiries and booked a pitch via email. I got the impression that out of the main holiday season, it wasn't so important to fill out forms or book way in advance in any case. For those preferring to roam about the countryside in their 'vans, chancing whether sites had vacancies, low season would probably be ideal. Still, a word of warning: certain events may be held in the low season, at a time when you'd think all would be quiet.

And, of course, there's the odd national or half-term school holiday to think of. This might mean that accommodation is fully booked-up or hard to come by last minute.

One thing I noticed was that each site divided the seasons up a little differently; hence tariffs would vary somewhat. Some sites also charge a flat rate per pitch, whilst others charge per person on top of that, with yet more fees for electric hookup, awnings and sometimes even for dogs. All in all, it seemed a good idea to confirm prices before travelling, since the wording on some websites could feasibly be misconstrued by the uninitiated.

Our site was set on one of the flatter moorland areas near the tip of the Cornish peninsula, not far from Land's End. After a friendly welcome at reception by one of the owners, we pitched up. The site was sparsely dotted with campervans, while some pitches had number-plates staked into the ground. It reminded me of how people hang coats on the backs of chairs to show they've been claimed and that the owners will be back shortly to sit on them.

Our leisure battery had been flat last trip, so up till now, we'd had to manage with lamps. But not tonight! Now, with the revolutionary power of electric hookup, we could easily illuminate our space, rather than fumble about in the half-light to set up our bed – we could even sit up in bed and read! (How easily pleased some people are!)

We could also now power the fridge using electricity instead of gas. Rolling into autumn, we'd been able to manage so far by placing cool-blocks inside before leaving home. This seemed adequate for a couple of days to chill basic dairy items like milk, cheese and butter. At night, we also enjoyed the fact that the on-board fridge was blissfully quiet, unlike our fridge-freezer at home. It didn't matter whether we ran it on gas or electricity, it was so soundless that we wondered if it had conked out; and we had to double-check the pilot light was lit.

We settled down for the evening, Steve with his book and me with paper and pen. Although I use a computer most days for my writing etc, we chose not to bring one along on our trip. There is something peaceful and simple about not being hooked up to every mod con and, as a writer, it's quite satisfying to have sheets of paper on my lap to scribble down whatever comes to mind. Somehow, I think the act of writing itself taps into a part of the brain that computers don't (or can't). Trouble is, I end up having to type up my travel notes when I get back home, and it always takes twice as long to do so.

Set in a sparsely-populated part of the country, we had a good night's sleep and woke up on the Sunday morning ready to spring into the day's activities.

Although I'd lived in this area of Cornwall years ago, I'd never got round to visiting Geevor Tin Mine, so off we went to find out a bit about Cornish mining history. Now, that might not sound enticing to some readers, but I *will* say that the more I visit places like this, the more I realise what a shoddy job my history teacher did of bringing the past alive and making it interesting.

Located on the coast near Pendeen, Geevor was, until the 1990s, a working mine, so wandering through the site, you really can get a picture of the past: where the ores were processed, where the miners worked, the engineering involved in getting them down to the shafts, and much more. An installation shows you how amazingly convoluted and far-reaching the network of mines is in the area (some going miles out to sea), and you also learn how far afield Cornish folk have travelled in the pursuit of mining over the years. There's also an interactive section, and you can even take an underground tour if you're game.

When visiting such tourist destinations, I'm often struck by the contrast between past and present. Here we are, modern-day tourists, barely aware of what a luxury it is to stop and stare at the beautiful views; whereas the folk working the mines years ago would have been in the relative dark for most of the day.

Although we had cooking facilities in our camper, we decided to indulge ourselves at the Geevor café. As we ate lunch, we noticed there were paintings hung on the walls which were done by a local group. Now, the artwork demonstrated a wide range of talents, shall we say; and, priced at a tidy sum, I wondered whether I ought to start painting again myself.

As with so many tourist attractions, you could easily spread your visit over a couple of days just to take it all in. But by late afternoon, we decided to go home and leave enough energy to unpack our belongings.

It was clear that, even a local journey could feel like you'd been away for weeks. *A change is as good as a rest*, they say! And it's certainly true.

With Steve at the wheel, my mind wandered as we trundled up the highway, and I couldn't help thinking about the artwork in the Geevor café. Perhaps I had picked the wrong profession, I mused. Hmm... *When we get home*, I thought, *I really must dig out those old brushes and paints...*

~ 3 ~
STRETCHING OUR WHEELS

Originally, we'd thought of taking a holiday to Greece late season. But with our campervan now on the scene, flights abroad would be shelved. Instead, we had dreams of sucking the marrow out of having the wherewithal to explore the world via road-trip (if you'll pardon the metaphor).

At first, the idea of going to France appealed. However, doing the sums, we realised that, far from being a cheap holiday, the ferry ticket alone (from our nearest port of Plymouth, over to Roscoff) seemed expensive, even for our current month of October.

Calculating an approximate mileage for a tour round Brittany in northern France, we realised that our relative gas-guzzling, two-litre engine would make the holiday more pricey than we would have liked. Add in campsite fees and you're looking at a tidy sum.

We were also having to pay out for some work on our home at the time, so all things considered, we'd have to holiday on the relatively cheap in England until I hit the big time with a bestseller – or got round to painting some major cash-generating masterpieces for the Geevor Tin Mine café.

We always seemed to get the most out of a holiday when we had something in particular we wanted to see or do. During a holiday in France a few years back, we'd visited several of the Dordogne's high concentration of caves, and this had whetted our appetite to see what caves were around Britain. Having visited a few closer to home, perhaps we could now look further afield and use cave visits as a focal point for our holiday.

A bit of internet research turned up some 'showcaves' in south Wales at a place called Dan-yr-Ogof. In effect, a 'showcave' is the fancy name for caves open to the public, usually after being worked to make them safer and more accessible. The other famous showcave in Britain, Wookey Hole, could easily be woven into a trip to Wales. It seemed like a good plan.

When it came to the nuts and bolts of how the campervan worked, I was a bit of a dud, so whilst Steve was making himself useful, attending to the more mechanical pre-journey 'van checks, I was busy in the computer-skills and organisation department, scouting out places to visit, campsite facilities, prices and availability, as well as printing up local maps and going over our checklist.

Having a towing caravan or dedicated motorhome (one not doubling up for other uses during the week) means you can have your 'stuff' all packed away ready to go at more or less a moment's notice. However, since our 'van was dual purpose (used both for holidays and travel to work), we had to unpack and repack the 'van between trips. It was a far cry from our original 'wild and free' dream where we'd jump into the 'van on a whim and head off to some unknown destination.

But by now, we'd begun to rough out a decent enough packing checklist. At least it would dispense with the time-consuming chore of thinking through what to pack for every trip, and help us avoid forgetting that one, all-essential item. We also stuck up a piece of paper in the 'van on which to write suggestions for things we'd find really useful to bring along, or jobs to do to improve the camper. We knew our memories were like goldfish's and that, once we were home, we'd forget all those bright ideas. (By the way: sorry, goldfish – you're probably much brainier than scientists give you credit for!)

We'd been on a couple of trips already now, and what was becoming clear was just how much 'stuff' we hauled around with us. Did we really need to take all these things along? Where was the simple life we'd aspired to by buying a campervan? It was clear you couldn't pour the contents of your home into such a small space.

When it came to packing, we were starting to look at what we *needed* versus what we *wanted* to bring along. With a smaller 'van, it was more important to stick to a 'campervan diet'. What could we do without, and what could we buy at our destination instead? After all, everything we had in the 'van before we set off would be weight we were paying to lug around.

Although it would've been nice to have a break from modern technology, I decided to bring my PC along this time. Typing up a few days' worth of writing was bad enough – this time, we'd be going away for over a week! And if we really fancied chilling out with a video of an evening, we had the option. Otherwise, our days would probably be so full, we'd have little time for such entertainments.

* * *

Perhaps I had gone a little overboard, but by the time we headed off on our trip to Wales, we had a well-organised folder full of research pertaining to our chosen destinations. Despite this, we weren't sure if we were going to stop off on our way up to Wales, or on the way back down: it would depend how early we set off and how well we were doing for time.

On our trip to west Cornwall, we'd had a taste of what we called *The Campervanner's Wave*, where fellow motorhomers would wave to us. But after only a short time of waving back, our arms were getting plum tuckered out – which raised a few important issues. In terms of inter-motorhome relations, what kind of message would we be sending by ceasing to wave? Could we be disappointing the enthusiastic soul approaching us in his Hymer? Or making a fellow 'vanner feel snubbed?

Equally important was the safety aspect of so much waving. I don't mean in terms of taking your hands off the steering wheel (which, of course, is a concern), but isn't there a serious risk of getting RSI (Repetitive Strain Injury) from the frequent lifting and waving of your hand?

Given these issues, one wonders where to draw the line. Do you suffer in silence whilst notching one up for good relations? Given our experiences, one certainly has to have some sympathy for the Queen, with her *Royal Wave*.

That said, the saying goes that necessity is the mother of invention, and it might not be impossible to invent an artificial hand to take over the gruelling task of hand-waving. And, for those of you who get irate with other drivers, I'm sure the hand could be designed to perform several gestures, should the situation veer from 'entente cordial', shall we say.

We were half way to Wales and it was getting on in the day. So, we detoured to Glastonbury with the intention of visiting Wookey Hole the next day (our contingency plan for a late departure from home).

Glastonbury, renowned for its New Age types and oft-flooded (or at least heavily rained-out) annual music festival, wasn't somewhere I'd ever been particularly fussed about visiting. Having lived in an area of Australia renowned for its alternative types years back, I'd probably seen enough flaky punters (having once been one myself) and crusty hair-dos to last me some years yet. Surprisingly, though, we saw not one rainbow-garbed, incense-toting bod. Had they all left after the main summer season? Or were they off building canoes in which to paddle round next year's Glastonbury Festival?

We spotted a camping sign on our approach. The only site in my parks guide was Old Oaks Farm at Wick, so we headed that way. In mid October, there were plenty of pitches on the farm site and, with the help of the two friendly staff, we settled in with a direct view of Glastonbury Tor and lowering sun.

A hot cuppa after our journey from Cornwall washed down the delicious carrot cake – apparently most popular with visitors – made by the site owners' daughter. Our site view as we sat in the camper was of well-manicured, grassed areas with gravel access ways; and many of the trees dotting the site had a profusion of apples sprinkled around the base. A squirrel was bobbing about exploring the area as we left on our late-afternoon walk up to the Tor, which was less than a mile from the site. With no adjacent parking for visitors, it was lucky we had a pitch within easy reach where we could leave our 'van.

The Tor dates back to the 15th Century and, according to one website, "Glastonbury Tor is home to Gwyn ap Nudd, King of the Fairies. In the human realm it is managed by The National Trust". Although this is the case, you don't have to pay any fees or be a member of the National Trust (or any Fairy Realm) in order to visit. In any case, with 360-degree views for miles over the three surrounding counties, it was well worth a visit, and we descended just as the sun began making its way below the horizon.

In most vehicles, a journey from Cornwall to Wales might be considered a jaunt easily done in an afternoon. However, with the combination of a late start (due to snail-paced packing), a not-so-powerful engine and a generally laissez-faire attitude, we were happy to let our stop-off to Glastonbury and Wookey be part of the overall journey. Better that than hurrying to our destination only to feel wrung out upon arrival. It was only on subsequent trips away that we met other motorhomers who wished they'd broken up their journeys and stopped off somewhere on the way, too.

Ask anyone to name a cave in England and the first place they'll probably think of is Wookey Hole in Somerset. From my prior research on the internet, I got the impression that its target audience was families, a hunch which was confirmed as soon as we arrived.

Not only were there guided cave tours, but a range of other fun-packed attractions to keep kids amused, such as the paper-mill, Victorian penny arcade and museum.

The first cave dive in Britain was made from here, in the Witch's Parlour in 1935 and twenty-five caverns have been found in all. Just as the River Axe runs through the caves, so too does the legend of the Witch of Wookey Hole. An outcrop of rock which (if you put the lights out!) could be said to have human-like features, is reputedly the remains of a witch turned to stone by a Glastonbury monk who splashed her with holy water. (Not the best of friends, then!) The constant temperature of the caves also makes it ideal for the region's maturing authentic Cheddar cheese.

As forty-somethings with no children to entertain, and aiming to be in Wales by the afternoon, we were only interested in visiting the caves, and headed for the exit after taking the tour. However, a bunch of large dinosaurs outside in the 'Prehistoric Ice Age Valley' caught Steve's imagination and slowed down our progress. Personally, I wasn't keen on standing there in the pouring rain while Steve tried dredging up dinosaur names from the murky depths of his flagging memory. Even though I could see the names hidden in the bushes, he seemed to get a kick out of trying to remember the 'less common' ones. I said earlier that I didn't have children, but with Steve around, I'm not so sure sometimes!

Instead of taking the road we'd come in on, we opted for what looked like a short cut on the map, and spent twice as long double-backing due to inadequate signage. Not a good move. In the end, we found our way back onto the main road and made our way to another country entirely: Wales, the supposed home of the leek…

~ 4 ~
THE WELSH LEEK CONSPIRACY

Before leaving on our trip to south Wales, I'd pulled out my book of soup recipes. With autumn setting in, a warming broth would be easy to make in the 'van and would be heart-warming in the colder evenings. What recipe would be more befitting to take along than one for leek and potato soup? After all, Wales was the home of the leek, so we should surely have no problem finding the ingredients during our trip.

As we drove through Swansea on the way to our campsite, we picked up petrol and provisions at the supermarket. I spotted a pre-pack of "trimmed British leeks" and thought better of buying laminated veg, deciding that, surely there would be some farms in the area where we could pick up some leeks. Well, what could be more tasty and eco-friendly than fresh, local produce, eh? So, we left the store leek-less, yet determined to support the rural economy, which I reckoned needed it more than the supermarkets.

A photo of a serene cliff-top ocean view in a motorhome magazine had inspired us to stay at the Three Cliffs Bay on the Gower Peninsula on the south coast of Wales, an area which is great for watersports, cycling and walking. According to the magazine text, in 2006 the Independent newspaper named the site as having the "number one best view from any campsite in the world". Unfortunately, by the time we got there, the view was almost non-existent, hidden behind impenetrable cloudbanks.

Would it be cheeky to offer to pay for our site based on the percentage of view we got? We'd be forking out what seemed like top whack to us, even in low-season October, for what amounted to a panorama of Scotch mist and mizzle. But the staff were so friendly, and the site an otherwise peaceful and well-appointed one, that we decided to hang the expense and go through with our plan of staying a few nights.

The site wardens, Ellie and Ian, were surprisingly chipper, given that they'd just weathered the main holiday season; and they were very helpful in giving us the low-down on the local area. They pulled out a map, more-detailed than the one I'd printed up; and we realised that having one would be particularly useful if we'd been staying around longer, or if we were ramblers who enjoyed exploring every nook and cranny.

Although we like to have a focus to our holidays, somewhere we would like to check out before we go, there are always lots of leaflets and brochures on display once you arrive at your destination, giving you ideas for other places to check out that you hadn't thought of. Plus there's always the odd sign you stumble upon as you're driving round which might direct you to an unexpected place of interest.

The 'van was cloaked in darkness as we ate our evening meal and, as it was perched a 'hop, skip and a jump' away from the cliff edge, the wind whipped up the rock face, buffeting our 'van from side to side – so much so that anyone looking from the outside might have thought we were up to no good.

As we set up our bed for the night, I got Steve to check that the handbrake was securely in place. With the peace of mind that the wind *probably* wasn't going to force us off the cliff overnight, we snuggled up with our duvet and hot-water bottle, and happily fell asleep to the sounds of lashing rain, feeling quite cosy.

The next morning, little had changed weather-wise. Sitting there in your metal confines, looking out onto the bleakness, you sometimes wonder what to do with your day. Taking a book to read is always a good idea, in case you really can't be bothered to face the bad weather. But, nine times out of ten, we found that, if we made the effort to get out there and do something in spite of it all, the weather often met us halfway.

After breakfast, we made plans to get our act together and head off for Wormshead (a peninsula on the Gower Peninsula, as it were). The landscape here reminded us of Cornwall, with sandy beaches and a rugged coastline that seemed to stretch for miles. Had we driven all this way to experience somewhere not that different from home?

The weather seemed just the same as well, 'windswept' being an understatement of our brisk walk. I bet if Steve had attached a piece of string to me, he could have flown me like a kite. Still, there's nothing quite like it to get your appetite going and make you appreciate the shelter of the 'van when you get back, by indulging in a restorative hot cuppa and warming lunch.

Parked next to us was a motorhome, larger than ours. Its rust-free, gleaming-white fibreglass shell made ours look shabby in comparison. Even so, we got chatting with the couple inside and, despite our 'lesser' campervan, I never got the impression they were looking down their noses at us. It seemed that by the mere fact of having a motorhome, we were 'in the club' so to speak; and they were keen to pass on a few tips to us 'newbies' about the often Mysterious World of Motorhoming.

According to our neighbours, you could get site discounts if you were a member of certain caravan or camping clubs. Not only that, but you could stay on cheaper farm sites with minimal facilities if you were a member. They enthusiastically pulled out a thick book packed with lists of sites. These cost only a few pounds per night, they said, and made our current site fees seem not only expensive but extortionate.

We were also told about cheaper sites in France. You paid a small annual fee to an organisation and could stay at farms, vineyards, and so on. Unfortunately, you needed your own washing and toilet facilities. All we had to rely on were the sink and porta-loo. Of course, they enthused, you could always 'rough it' on one of these sites for a few days, then move on to a fully-equipped site in order to empty your toilet, have a proper shower and top up water supplies.

The couple were being so helpful that the information whizzed by at a rate of knots. Which exact club were they talking about? Where could we get more information? We later discovered that they were referring to the Caravan Club in Britain (and its cheaper 'CL' farm sites) and France Passion respectively.

The couple had also travelled in Scotland and, as far as they were aware, it was legal to park in laybys there (unless otherwise signposted). In France, there was a whole network of off-road 'aires' (basically, 'parking places') where you could overnight in a motorhome (not a caravan or tent), use toilet facilities and replenish your water supplies. These are often free but sometimes incur a fee.

Even though aires don't have the facilities of campsites, we might have gone to France after all, had we known about these other options. It turns out that Vicarious Books can supply books about aires – which exist all over Europe – as well as information on France Passion and other overseas travel options – eg the ACSI card for site discounts (link at end of book).

Europe is an option worth exploring, especially if you are retired and have a decent amount of time to journey round. If you've plenty of money to throw around, then you probably won't be worried about shelling out for a large 'van or the ferry and fuel costs. However, if you're working to a budget, it's worth remembering that, the larger the 'van, the more it costs to get it over to the Continent. Free aires (and possibly a ferry discount via a club or other) could certainly offset fuel costs to a certain extent, too.

It's easy to forget just how spacious mainland Europe is in comparison with England, and motorhomes do tend to guzzle the fuel in comparison with cars. So if you have a rough idea where you'd like to travel, it's certainly worth estimating fuel costs, so as to avoid having a coronary on your return home as a consequence of receiving a credit card bill that's much higher than expected.

Some head off for places like Spain in the winter. There can, of course, be rain and snow down there, but you do have more of a chance of catching some sun and having higher temperatures there than in England. In America, many folk with large motorhomes or RVs (whether used as a true Recreational Vehicle or a place to live) flock south for the winter, earning themselves the name 'snowbirds'.

With a stomach full of lunch and a head full of information, we headed back towards our site and chanced upon a small farm shop. The sign at the bottom of the road listing their main fare didn't mention leeks, but there'd be no harm in taking a look. In the shop, I picked up a couple of onions and a Brussels sprout stalk and put them on the counter: "No leeks, then?" I enquired. "No, I didn't get round to putting them in till late so they're all tiny. We're just using them ourselves at home," explained the farmer.

I wouldn't mind some, even if they are small, I wanted to pipe up. But I remained politely silent. There was no offer to pop on his wellies and go harvest any for me and we drove back to the campsite leekless once more.

Browsing our map the next morning, we were tickled by the name of a place called Mumbles not that far from our site and couldn't resist a visit. The weather had cleared and was fresh and sunny; and from the coastal town we could see Swansea in the distance across the calm bay.

At the end of a relaxing walk along the seafront, we came to a lighthouse (not the type that's open to the public) sitting off Mumbles Head. We decided to explore the pathways on the small headland and, despite the otherwise calm day, once you rounded a corner, the wind whipped up and made you feel like you'd walked into another dimension.

On the way back to the campsite, we stumbled upon a sign for the Gower Wildflower and Local Produce Centre and followed it. Outdoors, there was free parking and a wildflower meadow, pond, roundhouse and willow igloo. And, as well as selling a range of native plants, there was an eco-friendly shop and café selling local produce.

Wonderful! I thought as we entered the shop. *I can buy the ingredients for that leek and potato soup now!*

Purchasing the spud half of the recipe, I queried with the chap on the till: "No leeks, then?"

"They're not in season yet," came the reply.

I paused, tactfully mentioning that I had a few early leeks growing at home which were probably about ready. Hesitantly, he admitted, "Well, we *do* have a *few* growing, but they go straight out to certain restaurants and Swansea market. They sell ten times as much as we do, so..."

He was a helpful bloke, but somehow, I didn't think he was about to pop out the back and dig up a few leeks for me either. We would again be walking away bare-handed leek-wise. *Spaghetti on toast for tea tonight, then,* I muttered as we went back to the 'van.

This was getting a little silly. All the propaganda and hype of my youth (mostly via the singing comedian Max Boyce, I hasten to add) pointed to Wales as a leek-abundant country – and *this* is what we get? It was like going to Cornwall and not being able to find a pasty. There had to be some conspiracy going on here. Were the Welsh reluctant to hand over their hard-won leeks to the likes of 'foreigners'? Surely, by now, I was starting to sound like the old TV character, Victor Meldrew, with my "I don't *believe* it!" complaints.

Back at our site, we decided to make the best of the day's remaining sunshine and set off for a walk on the beach down below our campsite. It looked so inviting that we couldn't have guessed, before we descended the steep access lane, that sand would whip up into our faces – so much so that we could barely see anything. Unless we developed an extra set of camel eyelids, we might as well leave, we thought.

On the way back, we visited reception to square our bill and, chatting with the assistant, discovered that the shower blocks were fitted with solar panels (we'd been too busy to notice), which meant that little or no gas was used to heat the water in summer. Coins operated the showers and, although some sites gave you a short shower time per coin, it did mean resources were saved.

Back at the 'van, Henry the site pheasant was wandering about on the lookout for grub, and we gave him a bit of bread before settling in and sorting out our own meal for the evening.

Leaving the Gower Peninsula the next day, we moved up to Powys, home of the Brecon Beacons. I was still determined to get some leeks and wondered if we'd be able to find some up there. Yet we saw not one farm shop sign as we drove to our next stop in the Vale of Neath. Were the famous leeks of Wales just a myth? Our holiday was moving along, and the temptation to buy some on our next supermarket stop-off was mounting. But we weren't giving in quite yet. There would still be time. *Patience is a virtue!* I reminded myself, gritting my teeth.

As we turned off the main road, trying to find the Aberdulais Falls tourist attraction, we realised our ten-plus-year-old map was 'unfit for purpose'. This wasn't the first time our ancient map had had us 'groping around in the dark in broad daylight'. Since it had been printed, many new bypasses, estates and roads had been built, thus leading the unsuspecting traveller (in this case, us) astray.

Generally, you might expect that a National Trust property like this would be well signposted and thus easy to find. Unfortunately, on a quiet Sunday morning, there was no-one around who we could stop to ask the way. Eventually, we back-tracked, found we'd gone right past the place a few miles back, and settled into the adjacent tree-lined car park to wait for the place to open.

Somehow, we discovered we were (as usual) out of the loop as far as the rest of civilisation was concerned. Apparently, the clocks had gone back the night before, so we bided our time by fuelling up on a cooked brunch breakfast.

With a reasonable entry fee and friendly staff, we were happy to find Aberdulais Falls was no huge theme park of a place. And, although this was a plus side for us, it was probably also the reason why we'd driven straight past it!

The site at Aberdulais Falls houses the remains of buildings which were used over the years for anything from corn-milling to copper manufacture and tin processing. A 'virtual reconstruction' of these buildings plus all-important waterwheel really brings the site to life, as do the videos of real-time workers filmed on site, producing tins for use in the canning industry.

The waterwheel is still in operation today and the Falls themselves have been (and still are being) used to power it, generating electricity for the site and returning excess to the grid – as per the National Trust's remit. Controversially, the Falls were dynamited in 1820 to provide materials for building work in Swansea. (Looks like there were a few conservationists around, even then.)

Whilst I can't blame many tourist attractions for incorporating a certain multi-coloured showmanship into their sites to increase footfall, the National Trust's formula was refreshingly simple, informative and retained the original atmosphere of the place. Although by late morning, the place was attracting families, it wasn't the sort of huge site where you could take the kids for a whole day's full-on entertainment. Still, I would certainly recommend a visit. The information provided was the right amount not to overwhelm, yet enough to spark your interest in the past and really bring it to life.

From Aberdulais Falls, we drove to the Brecon Beacons National Park – more specifically to Dan-yr-Ogof, The National Showcaves Centre for Wales. In contrast to Aberdulais Falls, Dan-yr-Ogof was much larger than I'd guessed from my research. But, since we enjoyed visiting caves, and there were camping pitches on site, it seemed the ideal place to stay.

The entrance area was bustling with parents and children kitted out in raingear and we were greeted by a gigantic dinosaur on the gate. It looked like a vegetarian, so we were probably safe to proceed, and found our way through the equally jam-packed coffee shop to sort out our campsite booking.

Arriving on an early Sunday afternoon, I'd somehow envisaged the site being pretty quiet. However, not having children ourselves, we were clearly out of sync with school holidays, our visit coinciding with the inevitable desperation of parents trying to find an entertaining place to take the kids on a wet Sunday afternoon at half-term. In the end, we booked into our pitch, settled in and had a late lunch, hoping the crowds would burn themselves out by late afternoon.

Our arrival back at the entrance for a tour was a quieter affair, although we'd left it pretty late to buy a ticket. However, our 'status' as pitch renters allowed us some leeway and the assistant let us finish off our tour the following morning, meaning we didn't have to zip round the attractions.

There are three showcaves in all to see: Dan-y-Ogof Cave, Cathedral Cave and Bone Cave. They're all different sizes and each has something unique to offer. Dan-yr-Ogof Cave is the longest, and guided tours have been replaced with an audio dialogue pumped out of speakers. Bone Cave, although physically the least impressive, has housed forty-two human skeletons over the years (at least, that's how many they've found so far). The magical features of the more spacious Cathedral Cave are shown off to great effect with the use of music and creative lighting. At the end of the cave, there's an archway for the enactment of wedding ceremonies – although, I did wonder how audible the marriage celebrant's voice would be given the noisy, gushing waterfall nearby. *"Do you take this man...?"...* *"Err... Y'what?"*

On the site, there are information boards aplenty, a working model of how limestone caves form, a small museum, and a display of Iron Age huts with models of people who might have lived in them.

On top of all this, Dan-yr-Ogof boasts one of the largest dinosaur parks in the world, clearly evidenced by the many prehistoric models tucked away behind ferns or by the river. We were given an impromptu, mini guide to dinosaurs from a youngster called Archie. Although his parents tried to hold him back from overwhelming us with his enthusiastic patter, he was determined to rattle off all sorts of facts and figures about the Jurassic and Cretacious periods and the different dinosaurs – all from memory. Amazing!

If all that wasn't enough, there's also a Shire Horse Centre plus fields and pens with goats, sheep, pigs, horses, llamas and rheas (I'm sure I've missed something out) as well as a Jurassic Kart centre.

Since shire horses were invaluable in the area years ago, an old stable had been creatively transformed to house authentic-looking displays and videos plus a 'guided tour' from Tommy the Dog (don't be fooled – he isn't real). One of the displays had a table with vegetables on it. "Look! I've found a leek!" I called to Steve. Finally, after all my searching, I'd found one. Steve came in, but neither of us knew whether to laugh or cry as we stared at the display. Was fate mocking us by handing us plastic 'stunt' leeks which couldn't be eaten? Perhaps it was time to forget all about trying to find any leeks for our soup – after all, our holiday was almost over now.

Up till now, we'd followed the beaten track laid down for tourists, but surrounding our campsite were hills that looked unexplored by most visitors. So, the afternoon before we left, we ventured off. As we climbed, a misty bank hung low enough to give the lofty views a haunting edge, yet the sky was clear enough for us to see for some miles. Down below, we could see our campsite, dotted with what looked like toy vehicles from where we stood. The rolling hills and trees filled the landscape canvas with vibrant shades of green, finally giving way to stretches of rusting bracken in the distance. We eventually found our way back to the campsite, discovering a stream along the way.

Later, we decided to do some washing. The small washing-up room we'd been using throughout the holiday seemed to double as a laundry room and was just big enough to house a sink for washing, and radiators for drying – but not spacious enough for a washing machine.

Unfortunately, we'd made the assumption that, because there were few *motorhomes* on site, there were few *people* on site. Apparently, there was a bunch of young army cadets tucked away on the grounds in their (no doubt green camouflage) tents. So when we went into the laundry room early evening to wash and dry our clothes, we were vying for sink time and drying space with one teenaged recruit after another.

The cadets got pretty active and muddy during the day. And it was obvious they hadn't picked up any laundry tips from their mothers, since their final rinse was still laden with thick, dark particles. Even after a morning out on his bike working up a good sweat, Steve's clothes never stank as bad as the clothes these guys were wearing – and that's saying something! The reeking emanations asphyxiated anyone who entered the small wash-room (ie us), but I wasn't about to give the lads a laundry lesson.

Radiators plastered the walls and churned out so much heat, you'd think they were powered by an underground lava flow. The sheer volume of badly-washed socks and still-half-dirty trousers took up nearly every inch of available drying space. Our own clothing might be in danger of absorbing some of the stench from the lads' pongy kit via steam osmosis overnight. It was a risk we had to take – but at least it would all be dry come morning!

Despite all this, having the radiators had been a godsend – not only for laundry, but also for drying our wet-weather gear. Walking in and out of our 'van with wet or muddy shoes, we'd also realised the benefits of having mats laid down. They saved the 'van carpet from getting dirty and could be removed and cleaned once we got home.

The last day of our trip to Wales arrived. Although we were heading back to England later that day, we stopped off at Brecon town, learning it was market day. Tucked away at the bottom was a vegetable stall, and we could hardly believe our eyes when we spotted a display of leeks. Were they fresh, local produce or tired imports? By now, my ethics were crumbling. I was like someone who's slept outside a department store overnight, desperate to buy a long-desired item in the sale. This would probably be my last chance to buy any leeks while we were in the country. Like the desperate sales shopper, I didn't much care about the price or where they came from. I just had to have them, whatever the cost!

Safe in the knowledge that I had my sought-after leeks, the weight I'd subconsciously been carrying throughout the holiday was now able to fall from my shoulders, and we idled about town for a while.

We spotted a camping shop, went inside and decided to buy a large, micro-fibre towel and two others made of some kind of moisture-mopping material. Even at sale price, the purchase set us back a pretty penny. We had no doubt fallen victim to some canny marketing – because at a later date, we spotted mini micro-fibre cloths (marketed as carwash cloths) being sold in a supermarket at a ridiculously low price in comparison. The material was barely any different, so we decided to try them out as mini towels – a 'first line of defence' after taking a shower. They could easily be washed straight away and ended up being much handier than larger towels which took up more space. And, since they were compact and dried quickly, the 'van avoided becoming a damp laundry house.

Our mini shopping spree over, we made our way out of Wales. Had we so desired, we could have spent more time there, touring round the Brecon Beacons National Park – half of which has been declared a Geopark. We picked up a leaflet for future reference which showed just how much there is to see and do in the area, including guided walks in summer. However, we felt like we'd had a good holiday; and we'd done what we set out to do.

We headed for my sister's in Bristol, with plans to stay a day or two before returning home to Cornwall. Upon arrival, she opened the door to greet us, and smells of home cooking wafted outside, warm and inviting on the late, overcast afternoon.

"What you got cooking, sis?" I asked, sniffing my way into the house.

"I thought I'd make us leek and potato soup for dinner," came the reply.

Now, I'm sure there's a moral in there somewhere, I thought. We search round desperately for leeks all week in Wales, then come back to England and suddenly find some without even trying. Hmm!... If I ever meet Max Boyce, I might just like to have a few words with him about his promotion of the Welsh national emblem.

Of course, the first thing my young nephew wanted to do when we arrived in Bristol was to go in our camper; and it was at this point that we realised just how much kids love campervans. To children, these places are better than theme parks. But three warnings I would give before letting them loose inside – especially if there's more than one kid involved…

Firstly, a Health and Safety warning: make sure you've switched the gas off and that there are no other dangerous things around. That's just sensible.

Secondly, you want your 'van to last, so be aware that kids will love to tug at, hang off, and swing on things as well as turn switches on and off ad nauseum as if caught up in a frenzy. Ask yourself how precious your vehicle and its various attachments are to you before inviting them in to break everything.

Thirdly, once kids get into your 'van, they won't ever want to leave. Tears and wails may ensue as you try prising them off the knobs, steering wheel, curtains and bouncy-castle bed. Be aware that, in the blink of an eye, your status will turn from the good-guy-with-the-fun-campervan to the wicked-witch-of-the-west-ripping-my-heart-out.

Now, to be fair, my nephew's behaviour wasn't in this league, but the 'campervan withdrawal tantrum' *can* present itself – and more so with kids who rarely see a campervan. Somehow, the novelty sends young minds wild; and, unfortunately, there is no cure for this, only prevention: if you can't handle the aftermath, don't let them in there in the first place. You have been warned!

Bedding down for the night on the street in our camper, we weren't sure how much sleep we were going to get, since we live in the country and are used to the quiet. So we were surprised that my sister's suburban dwelling, located not far from a main road, didn't have the constant hum that accompanies busy traffic areas.

Over the next few days, we managed to fit in a trip to Bristol town centre and a visit to Westonbirt National Arboretum not far away in the Cotswolds.

Although Westonbirt looks small on the map, it is in fact a 600-acre site managed by the Forestry Commission which showcases 16,000 trees (2,500 different specimens). I was taken aback by the eternal stream of people moving through. But, with the warm splashes of reds and vibrant oranges, it was little wonder: everyone was irresistibly drawn by the all-too-fleeting autumnal carnival of colours.

Our holiday ended with the firework hues of Westonbirt. And, with the rain and cold that were yet to come, our campervan dreams would go through a winter of their own, turning the blazing fireworks of our adventures so far to damp squibs – at least for a while...

~ 5 ~
DAMP SQUIBS & SNOWY ROOFTOPS

After our late holiday in October, it dawned on us that England wasn't exactly going to be a ball of fun weather-wise for the next several months. Many an opportunity for a weekend drive to a local beach was scuppered by squalling winds and lashing rain.

Once Christmas was over, Britain was hit by snow. Even if we had wanted to go away for a break, we were lucky if we could make it down the road, let alone go across country. Too many hills, too much compacted snow and black ice.

Still, the harsh conditions didn't seem to stop some fanatics from travelling. Judging by the pictures in some motorhome magazines, of 'vans cloaked in snow, some people loved going 'arctic camper-vanning' as we call it. *Was it a bizarre kind of sport?* we wondered. Or did people not realise it was an option to go abroad for the winter and chase the sun?

Even at the end of October, we'd found our trip to Wales pretty chilly – despite using hot-water bottles to pre-warm the bed, wearing woolly hats and jumpers, and rugging up with a mass of bedcovers! But, even if our Propex heater hadn't been on the blink, I'm not sure mid-winter campervanning was what got us all inspired.

Having said all that, our 'van was an older model, and it turns out that more modern motorhomes and caravans are more insulated (and probably have more reliable heating systems than ours). So perhaps it could be quite snug inside for some, after all.

Over the next few months, the snow shifted to a pattern of endless rain, not unlike that which we'd already had over past years. And, since we weren't holidaying in the 'van for the time being, it was easy to forget that it needed some attention over the winter.

Most noticeable was that the damp weather was worming its way into the 'van, making the seat blocks and blankets musty. We'd also noticed a few patches of rust starting to bubble up on the bodywork. If left unchecked, they'd certainly fester into bigger problems in the rain.

The skylight also appeared to have sprung a leak. This was enough of a problem in itself, but the knock-on effect was that the carpet by the back door was developing a damp patch. Despite putting a bucket and towel below the skylight, the moisture had already permeated up into the wood of the cupboard doors – and they'd started to swell and were hard to open.

And, to top it all, the on-board heater, which had worked fine at first, had more recently decided to be temperamental, coming on when it wasn't really needed and not starting up when we really could do with a bit of heat.

Was it an understatement to say we had our hands full? We might not be travelling anywhere for a while, but we certainly wouldn't be idle. It was just a shame that there weren't any 'campervan makeover' programmes on TV which would come in and magically solve all our problems!

Since the weather prevented us from leaving the 'van open to air it out, we brought the seat blocks indoors to dry out next to the radiators. We didn't think at the time, but we could also have tried putting a dehumidifier or fan heater in the camper – or some people put tubs of salt on the worktops to soak up excess moisture.

Some remedial rust work, a lick of touch-up paint, and a jolly good clean inside and out, transformed the campervan from rust-pocked, algae-harbouring ugly duckling to gleaming (albeit ageing) white swan.

The skylight was a bit more of a bugbear. Not quite sure how to solve the problem at first, we did a remedial patch-up job with a small sheet of plastic, which put an end to the troublesome drips for a time. But, being a 'bodge-it' job, the wet weather eventually softened the sticky tape, it peeled off, and water again seeped through.

Looking for answers, we remembered the 12 Volt Shop which we'd seen on a local market-stall before we bought the camper. We found they'd now relocated to a larger unit on a nearby industrial estate. Not only did they sell campervan accessories, but the shop was run by a couple, one half of which was a knowledgeable chap who looked like he could fix anything. He had his own 'van development project' on the go in his workshop and, although he wasn't touting for work as a motorhome mechanic, he was most helpful in fixing us up with a new skylight bought at his store. The only trouble was, the leak persisted.

Finally, we worked out the real source of the problem: there was a tiny gap between the skylight and the 'van itself; and since it had been so wet and windy, rain had managed to find its way in. Temporarily, we remedied the problem by levelling the 'van (it was parked on a slightly-inclined driveway), which at least stopped the rainwater from funnelling into the hole. Finally, though, there was a gap in the rain on one of Steve's days off work, and he was able to climb up to the 'van roof to seal it with silicon.

With the damp patch on the carpet and the swelling cupboard doors, we were lucky. The carpet eventually dried out – as did the doors, which surprisingly shrunk back down and became easier to open.

As for the heater, it was a Propex system that ran on gas. After playing around with it, Steve wasn't actually sure if it needed fixing at all. Because our gas bottle was low, he figured, perhaps there wasn't enough pressure for it to work. We later changed the bottle and the heating seemed to work fine again. Over time, we discovered that others – even those with more modern 'vans – also had trouble with their gas heating systems, so perhaps it was a generic problem after all.

All in all, by the time we'd got through that little lot, we could probably have put together our *own* campervan makeover TV show!

Having a water tank means keeping the pipes clean and draining it in winter to prevent the pipes from freezing up. (Unless, that is, you have an indoor tank not exposed to the elements.) So, given that we'd had enough on our hands already with the other jobs, we were quite glad that we'd opted early on to use one of those portable plastic containers with a tap (what Steve calls a 'carboy'), instead of filling the tank and pumping the water through the on-board taps. In any case, many people get on well enough with water tanks, and put in sanitizing tablets to keep the water free of bacteria. As I understand it, it's safe to drink the water from these tanks (so long as they're kept clean) but some folk prefer to drink from a separate container whilst using their tank water for washing hands and dishes.

Although we weren't using the 'van for holidays right now, Steve could still put it to alternative uses. For a start off, he could drive to his local cycle races. His bike could easily be housed inside the 'van whilst in transit, and it provided a cosy space to sit in, sup a hot drink or change his clothes after a race. Also, he could drive the camper to work on occasion and use it as a mini canteen in his lunch hour – a comfortable sanctuary away from his busy workplace. All this seemed to make up for the fact that the camper guzzled more fuel than our other vehicle. It also meant the 'van was having a run about now and then. After all, we didn't want it seizing up and giving us another problem to deal with, did we?

So far, we hadn't even ventured out for a daytrip together and, all in all, the colder, wetter months were a bit of a damp squib. Even mustering up the enthusiasm to dream a little and plan our next mini adventure was difficult. It was on a par with the challenge faced by gardeners looking outside in the depths of winter and having to rustle up the motivation to sow early seeds when the garden is at its most unglorified.

However, a few hours of decent sunshine on a February morning appeared as a font of inspiration which reignited our interest in making plans; and it looked like we just might soon be getting back on the campervan trail after all…

~ 6 ~
OUT OF HIBERNATION

Over the past few months, we'd toyed with the notion of getting shot of our 'van in favour of something more modern. After all, it was over twenty years old and we'd had a series of challenges to deal with.

The wetter months had made the cushions feel damp, the skylight had leaked, the cupboard doors had swelled, we'd found patches of rust, the heating was on the blink, and the jigsaw-style bed could be improved-upon. All of which could be rather off-putting to 'newbies' like us who started off without much of a clue.

An easier bed setup would have been nice, but that alone wasn't reason enough to buy a new 'van. And having dealt with the 'van repairs – at least as best we could for now – what seemed most important to address was whether or not the 'van was likely to pass the MOT test in a few months' time. A health check at our local garage confirmed the 'van was mostly in good shape. And, now that we'd gone to the trouble of doing all those repairs, why not keep the 'van – at least for a while longer?

Steve got it into his head to go back to the 12 Volt Shop and get a bicycle rack attached to the back of the camper. The idea with getting a double rack, he said, was that we could ride some of the cycle trails together occasionally when we went away. However, when Steve came home impassioned about the new rack, I found his enthusiasm highly suspicious. Since he'd been a fanatical cyclist for several years, I couldn't help wondering if he had an ulterior motive for getting it fitted. As a Cycling Widow, I should have known better than to fall for romantic notions of time spent together 'doing the trails'. With the cycling season imminent, Steve no doubt had it in mind to double up our holiday plans with his training regime and time trial races.

With time booked off in April, we were looking forward to getting away for a week of walking, taking photographs and viewing some lovely coastline a couple of counties over in Dorset.

By now gagging for a break away, we were disappointed to see a deluge of rain bucketing down as we looked outside our lounge window. And the forecast for the week to come was no different. We weren't going anywhere! A rain shower is one thing. Hammering, non-stop rain is another. So with such dire weather on the menu for our planned week away, we bottled out and plumped to spend the time at home instead. We'd probably made a good call because, for the rest of the week, we barely managed a local coastal walk on one of the days before the heavens opened up again.

Our rationale at the time was that we'd rather be indoors at home, where we could rustle up a roast meal and cosy up to watch a few DVDs rather than be stuck indoors in the campervan with few home comforts. But, in hindsight, might it have been all that bad? In reality, how easy would it have been to dry our clothing? Would the 'van have felt cosier than anticipated? Might the weather have cleared enough for us to get a few walks in despite the forecasts? Perhaps we would have enjoyed the opportunity to catch up on some reading, whilst popping out for a walk whenever there were promising glimmers of rainless grey sky between torrential downpours.

It wasn't as if we hadn't been away before in wet weather. Wales hadn't exactly been dry. But this was heavy, interminable rain – and we've only once had to brave such weather (in the year following on from this book). We walked round Trengwainton Gardens in Cornwall for an hour or two, suffered 'drowned rat syndrome', and did indeed find it difficult to know where to put all our wet gear in our small 'van. Staying on a site without drying facilities, we were lucky to have sunshine the next morning – which lasted just long enough to dry our clothes before the next downpour arrived. So if you have several days of wet weather and nowhere to dry your clothes, it'll no doubt 'dampen' the best-laid plans.

In any case, a few weeks later, we had a long weekend free of commitments when we could get away for a break to the previously-elusive Dorset.

Up till now, we'd picked up site information from park guides (old ones left in our 'van or newer ones that came as freebies with motorhome magazines) or by surfing the internet, but it was around this time that we starting considering the merits of joining some kind of club and staying on their sites. The two main clubs we'd come across were 'The Caravan Club' and 'The Camping and Caravanning

Club'.

It all seemed shrouded in mystery at the time, but since friends of ours were members of the Caravan Club, we decided to join. Without doing any research, it was kind of like pinning the tail on the donkey, but we thought "What the heck" and decided to review things once our year's membership was up. Now that we've delved into these things a bit more, it seems that the basic difference is that the Caravan Club is for caravan and motorhome owners, whereas the Camping and Caravanning Club deals with sites for those with tents as well as caravans and motorhomes.

Our Caravan Club membership entitled us to monthly in-house magazines. There are, of course, various motorhome magazines on sale at newsagents. Indeed, when we first had our 'van, we got them regularly. Nowadays, we only get them if there's something we particularly want to read, and the Caravan Club literature fills in the gaps, dangling regular 'destination carrots' and keeping us in touch with what's going on in the motorhome world.

We heard that the Caravan Club's main sites were clean and well-kept, with top facilities – a home from home – and could have quite a lot of pitches. Their Certificated Locations (or 'CLs' for short), which allowed a maximum of five caravans or motorhomes on site, were often set in rural locations away from the hustle and bustle, and were perfect for 'old duffers' like ourselves.

When joining a club, of course, you want to know whether it's going to be worth the investment. And, not only could the Club site discounts and lower-cost CLs offset the cost of membership, but to us, the value also lay in having access to the relative tranquillity of the CL sites.

With Caravan Club directory in hand, our excitement brewed about all the juicy possibilities that lay ahead for adventures in our campervan... and the heavy clouds soon began to part...

~ 7 ~
DAWDLING ROUND DORSET

On a Thursday morning in late April, with sunshine forecast for our first trip in the 'van since the previous October, the snow-laden and rain-soaked winter days seemed far behind us and our spirits were somewhat lifted as we packed to leave for a long weekend away.

With the help of our campervan checklist, we got our gear together easily within a few hours. Still, the list was gradually growing. We might have started off with the intention of simplicity, but it wasn't that easy to just up and leave on a whim with a handful of possessions. The job was made all the more difficult because Steve used the 'van for work back then, and we didn't want it loaded up with holiday stuff all the time. In the meantime, our challenge was to notice what we actually used and keep the list in check by crossing off excess possessions.

Even though we'd had the camper for a while now, I couldn't help clonking my head on the door frames as we packed the camper – whereas (taller) Steve managed to avoid them. It seemed to be a new sport I'd not only invented but could have won a gold medal for. It was probably a hangover from childhood, when I used to catch my head on the corner of cupboard doors which were just above my eye level. But, shy of taping cushions to every door frame (or strapping one to my head), I'd just have to be a bit more careful in future.

We had no major itinerary for this trip, although we liked the idea of going to Portland Lighthouse near Weymouth. Walking and exploring the area was what we enjoyed most, and we could always pick up bits of tourist info when we got to Dorset.

We also decided not to plan where we were going to stay. At this time of year, early season, we were bound to find a place easily enough (or so we hoped). So, armed with our Caravan Club directory, we'd just turn up at one of the Certificated Location sites (CLs) and see if they had a place to stay. There were plenty of them in the area, so we could always try another if a site was full, we thought.

From previous trips, we realised it was a good idea to note where the cheaper fuel stops were. The internet made it easy to find these and print up a map; and we'd be able to save money by avoiding the more expensive petrol stations.

Having set off, we got quite excited when fellow motorhomers waved (does that sound sad?). Whereas before, we'd grown weary of what we'd nicknamed *The Campervanner's Wave*, it somehow got us back into the swing of things after such a long break from being out on the road.

However, it was clear we didn't know where to draw the line in terms of who we waved to. What was the protocol here? No-one trailing a caravan had yet waved to us. *Did caravan owners only wave to other caravanners?* we wondered. Should we wave at VWs? Were they a sub-set of campervans, or were they classed as a-whole-nother fraternity of campers? Surely, to avoid straining your arm muscles at least, you'd have to whittle things down a bit.

Perhaps this explained why some drivers just didn't bother to wave in the first place... They were confused about etiquette, suffering from muscle fatigue, or the novelty had just worn off. That was understandable. What we hadn't considered at the time was: maybe our older 'van just wasn't swish enough for the likes of those who'd forked out a tidy sum for their 'van. Perhaps they looked down their noses at those of us with less expensive 'vans. Or maybe some campervan owners were just rebels at heart and not interested in belonging to the unofficial motorhoming fraternity at all.

As we entered Dorset that late-April afternoon, we were struck by the expanses of open farmland which contrasted with our 'native', verdant Cornish fieldscapes. Those fields which weren't covered in grass had been tilled, leaving a flat, orangey-yellow plot whose soil looked too stony to grow anything on. Yet, some kind of grasses or grains, along with rapeseed, seemed to be managing quite happily in some areas.

Since our trip to Wales, we'd bought an up-to-date road atlas to make sure we wouldn't get flummoxed by new interchanges and road layouts this time. Certain maps are also handy for pointing out local attractions – some of which aren't covered by the leaflets found in the usual tourist racks in pubs and other outlets.

Having said how useful a map is, if you have a larger motorhome or caravan, it's worth sticking to the directions in the Caravan Club's directory rather than take short cuts just because it looks quicker on the map. What the map (or indeed your GPS) *doesn't* tell you is the condition or exact size of roads. Sometimes, directions in the directory might look like they're taking you 'around the Wrekin' but they could also be ensuring you avoid hairpin bends or getting stuck down a hairy lane.

Time was getting on, and we headed for a site which also served food, at Charminster near Dorchester. Making our way up the drive to the Wolfedale Golf Course, we wondered if it might be a kind of exclusive site for golfers; but we were pleased to discover friendly staff and owners who looked like they didn't have a snooty bone in their bodies.

Unexpectedly, there were showers and electricity available, not mentioned in the Club's handbook. This meant the fee was £1 higher, but it was nice to have a hot shower – and one that wasn't token-based (and thus time-based) either.

The next morning, we got up in time for a fleeting visit to Cerne Abbas where, on a hillside, there lies the 180ft chalk outline of a naked ancient guy holding a club. As usual, no-one is really sure who he was, what he signifies, who originally carved him out or why. If the gent in question was meant to be a warrior of some sort, then he was doing so without armour – although his rather wieldy club and phallus were surely threatening enough to ward off any enemy of the time. Either way, the cold British weather doesn't seem to have affected the size of the gent's manhood. Not a sight for the faint-hearted, I urge the overtly prudish, as well as fragile ladies with heart conditions, to stay away.

We were getting hungry and looked through our AA guide for ideas, plumping for a quaint little village called Sutton Poyntz. As we drove, we couldn't help noticing another hill figure. This time it was the Osmington White Horse, cut into the limestone hillside in 1808, representing King George III. In contrast with our feisty Cerne Abbas fellow, he didn't appear to be naked.

We arrived at the Springhead pub before the main lunchtime crowd and would certainly vouch for the food (tasty and affordable), friendly service and lovely willow-tree views by the river, not to mention the ample parking with plenty of turning space for larger vehicles.

As we planned to move on towards Weymouth by morning, we

decided to make a visit to Durdle Door in the afternoon. After all, the rock archway *is* the icon of the Dorset coastline – the Purbeck Heritage Coast, to be more accurate. There are several types of stone to be found in the area – mostly famously, Portland Stone.

Barely had we managed a stroll on the beach before a lady slid awkwardly on some shingle. It was on top of smooth stone, so the area was deceptively slippery. Her female companions fussed about, trying to work out how bad the situation was and what to do for the best. As Steve's a fitness instructor well into his physiology, we went across to see if we could help.

The ladies turned out to be Swiss and luckily we were all able to muddle along language-wise. Steve got our 'beach victim' to reduce swelling by sticking her foot in the water and advised they move on as quickly as possible – once the swelling increased, she wouldn't be able to walk easily, and there was still quite a walk back up to the car park on top of the cliff.

Fortunately, on the way up, an ice cream vendor was able to ring for assistance. The lady was taken to the top of the cliff and Steve urged them to take her to the hospital to get her foot checked out. By way of thanks, one of the other ladies pulled a Toblerone chocolate bar from her bag and gave it to us – a token of gratitude which she'd probably brought all the way from her Swiss homeland. We gratefully received, feeling it impolite to tell her that we do actually have Toblerones here in England.

By now, we felt we'd had enough 'excitement' for one day and found a site at Buckland Ripers, near Weymouth. Adjacent to a small row of farm buildings and houses, our pitch had basic CL facilities plus rustic toilet. Our friendly farmer host popped out at some point to collect our site fees, and despite his friendliness, left us to our own devices otherwise, with only the cows mooching about in the neighbouring field for company. Some might prefer more social interaction, but after an eventful day, we were happy with peaceful stillness, having the small camping field to ourselves.

We loved the area's open spaces and wonderfully fresh air. And, whereas some might prefer clipped lawns on site, we thought it nice that the grass had been left to grow a bit. Such an environment is great for wildlife. There were clovers growing which would provide food for bees; and green- and goldfinches breakfasted on seeds or other in amongst the grass the next morning.

It was more out of curiosity and nostalgia that we visited Weymouth, our next destination, the following day. I'd been there about twenty years ago and wondered what the place was like today.

We parked the 'van in the port car park (you can catch a ferry to Jersey, Guernsey or St Malo from here) and strolled along the beach. The long stretch of fine sand was dotted with occasional crows rather than the usual seabirds and, after lunching in the sunshine on the seafront's Café Blue, we wandered about town. I had to wonder where the masses of people had come from. Were they tourists or just the usual Saturday shoppers? April wasn't usually such a busy time of year, except during Easter. As expected, there were the usual bucket-and-spade shops. And then we discovered the 'Fossil Beach' shop which not only sold jewellery but was also full of amazing fossils, shells, crystals and stones – even a mammoth's leg bone, or part thereof. In fact, it was more like a compact museum than a shop.

Another reason we'd gone to Weymouth was because it was a stop-off point for Portland Bill, a lighthouse situated at the end of a nearby peninsula. As we drove there, we saw amazing views over Chesil Beach – the beach that is said to be so fossil-rich that even someone with a visual impairment could probably find one. Fortunately, there wasn't time to stop off there and embarrass myself by discovering how bad I was at finding fossils. In any case, I was already more than capable of embarrassing myself in lots of other, more public ways, as it was.

We wound our way up a hill and Steve remarked that the view down across the sea reminded him of being back in Gibraltar. Our route took us past lots of quarries: the source of the famous Portland stone. It was funny to think that we'd left our home in Cornwall, where there are lots of granite quarries, only to find it had so much in common with our destination.

Finally, reaching the lighthouse, I could hardly believe it! It was uncanny how many times we'd driven to see a lighthouse, only to discover it was closed for cleaning or maintenance. And today was no different. To 'compensate', the car park fees were, for once, more reasonable than usual. It was hard to tell how close the mainland was, given the haze across the sea, but this only served to bring the bold red and white stripes of the lighthouse more into focus, along with the angular lines of the rocks framing the peninsula.

As we wandered by an ice cream outlet, it crossed our minds that the business must be a real money-spinner, especially with no direct competition. Even at this time of year, the headland was busy and, even if only a quarter of the people bought an ice cream, they must be raking in the cash. Hmm... We'd often thought our campervan looked like a glorified ice cream van. Maybe we should think about stocking up the freezer and selling some choc ices out the side window during the summer? The profits could be ploughed straight back into our 'campervan holiday fund'.

After a mooch round the lighthouse headland, we drove back from the Portland peninsula and spied the outlines of several navy vessels across the hazy water, their unearthly grey forms looming like innocuous ghost ships.

During the night, we heard what sounded like a speedway track in the distance. Fortunately, we'd listened to the radio that evening, and the British election debates had been in full swing. No doubt this had primed us for a deep sleep, and we turned over and fell back into the arms of Morpheus.

In the barn adjacent to our field pitch, the farmer had a bunch of old tractors and brought one out to work on with a friend the following Sunday morning. Popping over to chat, I learnt that 'rusty' was actually another word for 'antique' or 'classic', and that painting over the rust would be seen as devaluing the vehicle, since it would no longer be in its original condition. Something to bear in mind if I ever decide to invest in one, then! Some of the farmer's tractors were thirty or forty years old – which came as no surprise: not only were they rusty but the tyres looked like they were made from elephant skin.

It had rained overnight and the outlook was uncertain for the rest of the day. As we packed up, Steve pulled his trainers out from under the 'van where he'd left them to air out overnight; and even though he thought they were far enough under to avoid the drip-line, the rain had still managed to dampen them.

As we made our way home, fog obscured what would otherwise have been fantastic views of the coast. Grey skies began clearing as we neared Cornwall, only to fill again with rain as we reached home. Despite all this, we reminded ourselves we'd had some terrific weather while we were away; and considering how few days of sunshine we seemed to have had over the past several years, even in summer, it was something to be grateful for.

A few weeks after our mini holiday, we received an email from the Swiss ladies we'd met at Durdle Door. Although Steve had advised them to take their 'beach victim' to the hospital, they hadn't. When they got back to Switzerland, they got her checked out and it turned out she'd actually broken a (non-supporting) bone in her leg. Remarkably, despite the pain, she managed to get about for the rest of their holiday without doing herself any more damage.

No doubt, since this lady was abroad, she didn't feel comfortable seeking out a hospital in an unknown place. But if you're overseas in your motorhome and think it's not worth seeking medical advice for something that crops up, then this is a good tale to remember. Things could easily have turned out much worse.

~ 8 ~
PEAK EXPERIENCES

Sometimes you have a vague idea of what you'd like to do when you go away. Other times, you just head for a destination and see what happens. For our trip to the Peak District in the middle of May, I did a lot of destination research, but none with regard to accommodation.

Whether you're into walking, watersports, cycling, general tourist attractions – or even events like motorhome shows or rallies – basing your trips around an area of interest can help whittle down where you'd like to go. Before we got our 'van, we'd listed places we'd like to visit, and things we'd like to do at some point. Referring to the list whenever we planned a trip, we'd gradually worked our way through the bulk of it. And now we were off to Derbyshire, which we chose because of its high concentration of (yet more) caves open for public viewing.

As a keen gardener, this was a crucial time of year for nurturing seedlings, so before we went away, we asked an old neighbour if he could give them a regular check and water. "No problem!" he said keenly. He'd apparently been a head gardener once (so he said), and was always outside in his own garden, so I should be able to leave for the week, safe in the knowledge that my burgeoning tomato plants would be well tended.

Before heading off, Steve checked the basics like tyre pressure, oil and water. A few hours into our journey, the Navigator-by-Default (me) realised all too late that (S) on the route map meant 'Services', and we missed the turn-off for mainstream refreshments. Just as well you can stop pretty much anywhere in the camper (although, of course, not on the motorway's hard shoulder!).

By the time we reached the end of the motorway, we'd been responsible for wiping out several communities of flying insects, as we drove into them at high speed. We even had to put on the window-wipers – which were pretty choked up by the time we reached my sister's home in Bristol. I may not be a Buddhist, but I'm certainly not keen on killing animals, large or small; and I couldn't help thinking that my efforts at being a vegetarian, in order to preserve animal life, had just gone down the proverbial plughole.

We decided to break our trip into two parts, camping outside my sister's in Bristol on our way up north. We joked that my sister should set up a mini Caravan Club CL site outside her home, providing water via a hose and putting bollards out in the road to hold spaces for motorhomes, since parking is on a first-come-first-served basis in her small cul-de-sac. I could just imagine someone trying to reverse their caravan down the tight little street!

After our brief overnight stop-off, we headed north around midday, reaching Derbyshire by late Saturday afternoon.

With no accommodation booked in advance, we looked in the Caravan Club directory and drove to the nearest CL on the off-chance of finding a pitch. It looked like it had a few more motorhomes on it than are technically allowed (five maximum) and, at a glance, it looked just a little more 'laid-back' than we would've liked. It wasn't even that late and there were already plenty of beer cans in hand. My mind flashed to scenes of raucous frivolity by nightfall and I envisioned us – rightly or wrongly – getting no sleep at all. I blatantly admit to being a premature old fogey who cherishes her sleep – or what was called 'beauty sleep' in my parents' day – although, not sure that getting my forty winks has really done me much good in that regard. Perhaps it was a ruse all along, on my parents' part, to get me to go to bed early when I was young.

One thing we'd noticed from the Caravan Club directory was that, when searching under town names, there's a lot of area overlap. For example, several farms which were within a short distance of each other could be listed under either Buxton, Ashbourne or Bakewell. So you needed to check thoroughly under more than one town name. Eventually, we phoned round and found a site that had somewhere for us to stay – Westwood Field at Hulme End – situated between Ashbourne and Buxton.

All in all, it seemed that planning ahead not only took the uncertainty out of finding a pitch but also saved time sifting through the directory late in the day. If site owners weren't in when we phoned or turned up on site, we might have to find somewhere else to stay at the last minute. Perhaps our 'fly by the seat of your pants' wild camping dream wasn't all it was cracked up to be after all. Although pre-booking could be seen as a restriction, it ironically meant we'd be freer to enjoy the *sights* – instead of spending time worrying about the *sites*.

Arriving on site at Hulme End, the owner's son asked us what we were planning to do whilst visiting Derbyshire and, learning that we liked caves, he told us of a local walk in the nearby village of Wetton, where you could find Thor's Cave right alongside the Manifold Valley Trail.

Several of the National Park trails in the area run along old railway tracks and have been made suitable for cycling and walking with the help of tarmac. My research before we left home had only turned up the Tissington Trail (obviously one of the better-known ones), but not for the first time would we have a good example of how you can turn up at a place knowing nothing, and end up being directed to areas of interest with no effort or planning at all.

The site fee was £1.50 more than stated in Caravan Club directory. Although these changes could be seen as a bit of a gripe, the Club directory is printed only every other year, making fees difficult to keep on top of (although more current info should be on the Club website). The directory does also cover itself by mentioning that sites have unforeseen costs to cover and warning that the stated fees are the minimum charged. It's also worth checking fees before arrival and having the right money ready to pay in case a site owner doesn't have change.

Even though our site facilities consisted only of the basics required by the Caravan Club (water plus chemical waste disposal), we happened to have a field to ourselves and a green, spacious view. What we also liked about some of these CLs in contrast to the more 'swish' Club sites is the fact that the area surrounding your 'van is often not lit. Obviously, this will put some people off and it does mean keeping a torch handy. But since our 'van doesn't have the light-fast blinds of many modern vans, outside lights can seem more like floodlighting.

It didn't look like we'd have time to explore the Manifold Valley or Tissington Trails while we were in the area, but we did manage to fit in a walk to Thor's Cave before lunch the next day at the local inn. According to the information centre for the Manifold Valley (located near the inn), there were other small caves around, although they couldn't guarantee they'd be safe to go in.

With a name like Thor's Cave, you might envisage a spacious rocky recess befitting a mighty Thunder God. As it turned out, it was more like a grotto acquired by Thor's younger brother as a country renovation project – one he hadn't managed to spend any time on yet. The small cave was quite slippery and uneven to enter, although Thor's younger brother obviously had good taste when it came to picking places with a nice view, because it certainly was lush and green, overlooking the Manifold Valley.

Lunch equated to decent pub grub at the Manifold Inn. As we sat waiting for our meal to arrive, we noticed an advert on the table showing very nice guest rooms owned and let out by the pub, charged at £65 per night; and it occurred to us that, even staying on a more swish, full-facility site for a few nights could leave us with change from £65.

Deciding to get a campervan – instead of staying at Bed and Breakfast establishments (B&Bs) – seemed a good approach to holidaying and had its obvious financial perks. Having said that, there's nothing quite like treating yourself to a hotel or B&B holiday once in a while, just to make yourself feel pampered… No beds to make, no washing up or cooking to do. And, as we don't have a TV, staying in a hotel or B&B can feel like a real treat, even if most of the channels have endless re-runs of *Friends* and shows trying to flog you (allegedly) tacky jewellery items.

We headed off to Buxton mid-afternoon. Straight, well-made rock farm walls framed a number of fields sprawling with dandelions. They looked like masses of tiny sunlight bursts swaying in the breeze; and there were so many in the area that we had to wonder if they were farming them to make dandelion coffee.

Poole's Cavern was one of the formal 'showcaves' I'd researched before setting off; and the difference between caves like this and ones like Thor's Cave, is marked. Being open for public viewing, showcaves are usually much more pleasant and safe to walk around, larger in size (often 'chiselled out' for ease of movement), and have tour guides. Therefore, a fee is charged.

Parking had cost us nothing in the small car park at Wetton (a great surprise these days) and, although Poole's Cavern charged a meagre pound, we side-stepped the fee by parking in the spacious residential area right by the entrance.

Our philosophy of avoiding paid parking wasn't without its failures, however; and by the end of our holiday we would have experienced our fair share of the Pay and Display God's wrath – that which vehicle owners seek to appease with golden coins in order to evade His punishment via almighty parking tickets.

Perhaps we were just cheapskates at heart, but we could never really get to grips with the British institution of paid municipal parking. Whenever we'd been to France, there had always been ample free car parking, which encouraged people into town to spend money – either as a local or as a tourist. Surely the poor old Brits paid enough in Council Tax as it was to warrant a bit of free parking?

Poole's Cavern is your 'standard' limestone cave and claims the record for having the world's fastest-growing stalagmites (in case you forgot, those are the formations that grow from the ground, not from the roof). Just about every cave has at least one unique feature which is pointed out to tourists. This cave had two. One was the pièce de resistance at the end: an unusual and large shiny calcite rock formation. The other was what the tour guide described to us as 'poached egg' stalagmite formations. This description of the numerous erect stalagmites couldn't have been farther from the mark. Apart from the fact that each calciferous formation was unusually topped by a beacon of dissolved red iron oxide (which was supposedly the yolk), none bore any true resemblance to poached eggs. And had no children been present, I'm sure someone would have pointed out that the place looked more like a den for pagan phallus ceremonies or a repository for ancient 'marital aids'. Personally, I felt sorry for the young tour guide, who was surely no more fooled than we were, no doubt cringing every time he had to deliver the rehearsed line he was obliged to tow to cave visitors. In fact, I felt so sorry for him that, at the end of the tour, I gave him our saved car park quid (talk about generous tippers, eh?).

We spent the next two nights at Losehill Caravan Club Site, Castleton, in Derbyshire's Hope Valley, since it was best placed for the caverns on our 'to do' list. The owners were friendly and welcoming, and the site was immaculate with full facilities.

On our first trips away, we'd relished the thought of making a cooked English breakfast in the morning, but we were now going through a health kick phase, and ate porridge for breakfast. In terms of organisation and space, this was also a better option. The ingredients took up less space, and it was much quicker to prepare and clean up after, meaning we could set off earlier to get the most out of our day.

Monday's itinerary was to try and fit in a visit to three local caverns located within a short distance of each other: Speedwell; Treak Cliff; and Peak Caverns. We'd leave Blue John Mine till Tuesday.

Speedwell and Peak Caverns were twinned – since they were owned by a mother and son (the Harrison family) – so we could buy a joint ticket to visit them. We also got a £1 refund off our parking ticket.

Now, Speedwell, our first cavern visit, I'm afraid completely contradicts what I said earlier about showcaves. Many showcaves have room for tourists to manoeuvre. Not so with Speedwell Cavern, which is not for the faint-hearted or claustrophobic, since it involves a subterranean boat trip with very low ceilings. The network of tunnels eventually meets up with Peak Cavern; and despite an attempt to mine lead here, money was lost in the process.

We eventually came up for air (and light) and set off for Treak Cliff Cavern, which had lots of flowstones (limestone formations that look like water running in slow motion). It is the only place (apart from Blue John Cavern) where the famous Blue John stone can be found in the world – although a stone of similar chemical makeup exists in China. Treak Cliff is still mined, as evidenced by the shop which was filled with the stuff, and owned by a branch of the Harrison family.

Fortunately, we had our tour guide pretty much to ourselves – some tours can be packed and you sometimes miss what's being said. In any case, the only two others on the Treak Cliff tour just happened to be caravan owners staying on the same site as us and, as the tour ended, we stood outside for a chat.

Our vantage point took in the whole area, and we could see a giant building that looked like a factory in the distance. It was the same monster eyesore plonked in the middle of the countryside that we'd noticed driving through the day before. Since the couple we'd met were fairly local, they could tell us it was the Lafarge works, formerly known as Blue Circle Cement. Apparently, it had caused a bit of an uproar when it was going through the planning stages. The large, creamy-coloured building hardly blended in with the landscape; and I couldn't help notice that its outline looked almost like a fist, with the chimney stack extended as if it were a middle finger gesticulating in defiance to the locals. Obviously, no-one in the Planning Department had noticed this feature at the time – or, if they had, were happy to ignore the symbolism.

After lunch, we visited Peak Cavern. Also known as The Devil's Arse, we were surprised such a name had got the thumbs-up, given the British climate for politeness and political correctness. However, it turned out that the name went back many years and refers to the sound made in a section of the cave when water suctions through like a vacuum. Unfortunately, we missed out on a sound bite.

There was a demonstration of hemp rope-making at the entrance and we learnt the cavern had been mined for galena (lead ore) in the past, although it morphs into a limestone cavern in areas with stalagmites and stalactites.

What was most amazing was hearing about yesteryear's cavern tourism, which involved lying flat in a small, coffin-like boat whilst being pushed along by the guide who held a candle, probably in his teeth as he waded through the cavern water. The tunnels then were not that high and were 'developed' with dynamite only when Queen Victoria was due a visit. A monarchic nudge was apparently all the impetus needed to transform the cavern into a user-friendly showcave.

Driving through the area, you couldn't miss Winnats Pass, which runs like a gigantic crack between hills. As a long-term Cycling Widow, I'm used to Steve seeing every such geological feature, not so much as a thing of natural beauty, but more as a cycle training opportunity. He immediately deemed Winnats Pass as a great road for pedalling up and down, and decided to pop out for a ride before our evening meal. After all, he still had training to do for race events while we were away and, despite the fact that this was meant to be a lovely little holiday for just the two of us, he couldn't help bringing along his 'other woman' in the form of his bicycle strapped to the newly-fitted rack.

Back at the Caravan Club site for the evening, we wandered round and saw that it was quite full. Even though we weren't yet into the main British summer holiday season, it was no doubt popular due to its proximity to the local concentration of caverns, Mam Tor and neighbouring hills.

Most holidaymakers took up two or three pitches of the size allotted to us in our smaller 'van. One pitch was for their motorhome, the second for their marquee-sized awning, and if they'd come in a caravan instead, the third pitch was for their car. Some of the rigs were amazingly long and we wondered how the owners fared, manoeuvring them round the narrower lanes.

Several caravan owners had bird feeders on poles – some holding as many as three or four feeders packed with tasty bird goodies. It occurred to me that there would be birds back in their home garden, wondering where their favourite grub had gone while they were away. Subjected to an enforced diet, they would no doubt defect to a neighbour's garden until they returned... Although, these days, there seem to be so many feeders around that birds are probably in danger of succumbing to the same affliction as humans: twenty-first century obesity.

Steve and I had always thought campervanning was about minimizing your possessions and getting away from your usual surroundings. And yet it's clear that some enjoyed replicating their home life whilst on holiday, packing the proverbial kitchen sink. Who had room for bird feeders in their 'van? Certainly not us, in our Transit-sized vehicle. No wonder people needed such big rigs!

Doubtless, all of the caravans and motorhomes pitched up would have had a bathroom with a toilet and shower. Had we these facilities ourselves, we would've opted to stay on CL sites overall, paying a fraction of the price for a pitch. After all, we liked the less bustling sites and didn't see the point in paying to use facilities you already had on board.

We found it an interesting phenomenon, that folk had such big vehicles yet baulked at using their own facilities. One or two friends said they'd stayed on such sites and had never used their facilities either. What was it that put them off? The thought of having to clean out their toilets more often? Or jostling about in a more restrictive motorhome shower cubicle, after which they'd have to empty the grey-water? Or were we perhaps on the wrong track entirely? Did some people just prefer these sites because of the social appeal – a kind of like-mindedness or companionship factor?

Looping back round to our pitch we noticed a dog-walking area.

Deviating from this designated area (and leading your dog towards a nice, leafy verge instead) was pounced upon almost immediately. At first glance, it might have seemed a bit heavy-handed, but quite frankly, I was glad to see the site owners aiming to maintain high standards, given that I'd had my fair share of doggie-dooed shoes in the past.

The only CL sites I could find available for the next few days had minimal facilities, so we had a good scrub down and hair wash come the evening, and washed a bunch of flannel towels which we put in the drying room overnight – a great facility, especially in wet weather. While we were on an all-facility site, we might as well make the best of it.

While Steve went off for his shower, I spotted a couple of ducks wandering about. Did they belong to the site owners? Or had they got there under their own steam? It wasn't the first time I'd come across birds on a site. Back at Three Cliffs Bay in Wales, there was Henry the site pheasant. Now here were a couple of ducks milling about. I imagined they hadn't been able to reach the bird feeders and were scouring the site for alternative food donations.

The next morning, we headed off early to Blue John Cavern. I'd been on a school visit here years back and was keen to see if my memory of it matched reality. The first tour of the day, things were quiet, and we had the guide to ourselves.

One impressive area showcased a lode of the Blue John stone plus calcite. And 'churt' – some other solids we noticed in the cavern – are mined proper by some companies. The cave was drier than others in the area and it apparently never floods. Although it was mostly spacious, you had to watch your head in some areas; and I wouldn't recommend the numerous steps to older folk.

At Treak Cliff, we were told that Blue John (purportedly from the French 'bleu et jaune') had all but mined its last stone, but here, we discovered mining was still going on – albeit on what looked like a small scale. The mined areas are difficult to access and, due to Health and Safety, these are off-limits to visitors.

Leaving Blue John, I realised that I was only in my early forties and my long-term memory was already shot to pieces. I couldn't match my small wisp of childhood memory to anything I saw there, although I can still remember the piece of stone I picked up as a child outside the cavern, which I kept for years. Well, I *think* I can remember it, anyway!

In contrast to most places, the Blue John Cavern parking was free. Almost everywhere you looked in the area, there was evidence of our nemesis: municipal Pay and Display parking. And I mean everywhere. There were that many paid-parking spots snaking out of Castleton village, that I thought they were going for a place in the Guinness Book of Records. Certainly, the Council's Head Bean Counter must've been avariciously wringing his hands at the guaranteed money-spinner. Whilst these fees might not amount to much for the odd day, if you're on holiday for a week or two, they can amount to a tidy sum; and these have to be factored into the price of your holiday, especially if you're on a budget.

Having said that, the caverns that did charge for parking refunded some of the charges once you bought a ticket; although I did wonder why they didn't just charge you less to visit the caves in the first place – no doubt a portion of your ticket would go to funding the bureaucratic paperwork mill run by the Establishment.

Being able to prepare meals in your campervan is a great convenience, and we decided to bask in the luxury of a free parking space for a lunchtime snack, before heading off to a suitable parking spot for a walk up Mam Tor, the most notable peak in the area. Rather than take the easy route up the mount, we went up a particularly sharp incline that beckoned to be climbed.

Apparently, Mam Tor used to be a hill fort – not surprising, given its high vantage point. From the top, there were far-reaching open views taking in the neighbouring hills. Walkers passed us by, and there were more in the distance, following the ridges from peak to peak. Finally, we took the gentler route down and found the ubiquitous information plaque at the bottom, illustrating the hill's history. We spotted a few orange-tip butterflies; and, looking around, some areas brought images of Australia to mind, with clear blue skies and sheep dominating the grassy landscape.

By early afternoon, we'd had a decent enough walk and knocked a trip to Peveril Castle (walkable from town) on the head, making our way instead to our next site at Litton. In any case, we'd seen many a castle ruin in our time, and I always found it curious how organisations could get away with charging visitors *full* price for seeing only *half* a building.

Driving through villages, we were struck by the fact that so many had convenience stores; and, for campervanners, they certainly are convenient. They often aren't as costly as one might expect, and you can pick up a few gap-filler items without using costly fuel to drive further afield to find a supermarket.

Truth be told, I think avoiding supermarkets for at least some of your holiday can't be a bad idea. You might go into one with the intention of buying *only* what's on your list, but if you succeed, you either have a strong will or are in a tremendous hurry. Because supermarkets are obviously designed to suck you in and spit you out, having spent two or three times as much as you originally intended – thus encroaching into your previously-on-target holiday budget. Of course, you still run that risk with a convenience store, but since you're usually rushing in and out, the danger is lowered.

Back on the road again, we spotted gliders flying around nearby. Obviously, with all these hills around, they were well-placed to get plenty of lift. A sign pointed to a gliding club, and as Steve used to fly gliders, we followed it, hoping to get a closer look. However, the club house looked closed and, after watching a few gliders take off and land on the airfield, the novelty wore off and we carried on to our site.

At only a few quid, we wondered if there might be something wrong with the site in the almost-drive-through-without-noticing-it village of Litton. But it was actually fine – just basic. Although it had water on tap, we couldn't find the chemical disposal area – so it was lucky we'd emptied our porta-potty at Losehill.

Despite having had a good, pre-emptive scrub-down at our site the previous night, the walk up Mam Tor had gotten Steve all hot and bothered. I coaxed him to soak his feet and ditch the smelly socks. He thankfully obliged! Such close quarters can certainly put love to the test.

Sheep came in our field for a visit the next morning as we had breakfast. Having failed to find a site with shower facilities that had availability over the next several days, I put my mind to possible alternatives… Would it be just a little too cheeky and dishonest to sneak in to another campsite on the way down and use their shower?

We thought so. What about paying for one at a local sports centre? That would be an idea if there was a centre around, I thought, as the sheep moved on to the next field.

Personally, I could manage without a full shower for a few days, having had to fall back onto bucket-and-sponge washes when I lived in a canvassed dwelling in Australia. These were fine for taking care of basic hygiene in warmer surrounds, but not the sort of thing to resort to if camping in the colder British months. And you can, of course, always wash your hair indoors using the old-fashioned head-over-sink method if necessary.

That said, not all motorhomers are willing to 'sink' to the basic levels of living. Some aren't happy to use CLs – even ones with shower facilities. They want top-notch, full-facility sites every time – it's what some call 'glamping' (glamour camping). Nothing wrong with that – it's just a case of knowing what you're happy with, and planning accordingly. If you want the 'luxury sites', you have to check they're available before you go away.

We were now on our way to the Matlock area, home of (yes, yet more) caves, and stopped off for a fleeting visit in Bakewell.

On the high street we found a camping shop and couldn't help being drawn in for a browse. The shop assistant informed us that a new shop of this type appeared in the town every year. Was it my imagination, or did I detect a trace of bitterness in her tone? My mind did its usual thing of running to unlikely, wild scenarios, and I imagined her shop as having been the *original* outdoors shop in town. Opening it with pride, she'd felt like she'd cornered a niche in the market. But as time went on, others had cottoned onto the idea and she'd been overrun by competitors, some catering to the true trekker, others to wannabe travellers who like to adorn themselves in fashionable-versus-functional camping gear.

We left the outdoors shop not knowing what to make of her comments, but as we wandered round, two more camping shops lured us in before it dawned on us that the town might have cast a spell over its tourists, (allegedly) enchanting them with their wickedly-low offers and price reductions on super-soft, anti-pill, fast-drying fleece tops that even the strongest of wills would be hard-pushed to resist. Never before had we seen such a coven of these shops.

Our only hope of distracting ourselves from the evil lure of these shops was to duck into a bakery. We chanced upon a quaint little shop selling authentic Bakewell puddings – at least that's what the Italian owner said they were. The recipe apparently came about by way of a 'happy accident' and they are not to be confused with Bakewell tarts, which are different again. We couldn't resist buying one, and wondered if the seductive spell wasn't confined to the camping shops but to the whole town.

By the end of our visit to Bakewell, I was convinced that the place had more outdoors shops than it did bakeries (for which it was supposedly more famous); and in recognition of this, I suggest a town renaming, from Bakewell to Campwell, with 'a blur of camping shops' adopted as a collective noun.

Free of Bakewell's allure, we lunched in Matlock Bath car park, home to the famous Heights of Abraham, with its alpine-style cable cars and caverns. It was a hot day, so we tucked ourselves away at the shady end of the car park. We wouldn't have time to make our trip to the Heights that day, so we needed a 'filler' activity for the afternoon and referred to our AA guide for ideas. Although we hadn't so far done a whole walk or cycle ride from it, we'd used the information instead to suss out pubs for decent grub, hook up with interesting villages or do part of a walk.

So it was that we picked Bonsall, a small village nearby, and found our favourite kind of car park – a free one – before walking part of the circuit from the guide: a loop up through the wood and churchyard and back past some fields.

On our way back, I saw from a distance large letters on the side of a van which read "Blood Brothers". *How evocative*, I thought. Were these the type of guys seen in cowboy movies, who cut their palms before shaking hands and becoming blood brothers? Perhaps instead they were local butchers. From the depths of my memory came an image of the Mullarkey Brothers from my home town. They were tall, thin, bespectacled identical twins who ran an apparently-innocent, fresh fish shop. Were the Blood Brothers their Bonsall equivalent? Or was there something more dastardly afoot here in this backwater village – the kind of something that would make tasty fodder for a medical thriller novel?

As we neared the van, my untamed imagination was put firmly in check as I took in the Blood Brothers' other writing on the side.

Apparently, they were innocent chimney cleaners after all... *Or so they would have us believe*, I thought.

Returning to the car park, we noticed a row of recycling bins. I took over our recyclables and was amazed at the wide range of plastics it collected – not just the standard HDPE (category 2) that milk containers are made from. It probably sounds like I'm getting onto an environmental soapbox (made, of course, from wood sourced from sustainably-managed forests!), but I'm always surprised at the British recycling facilities – or lack thereof. Back in Australia where I'd lived some years ago, they recycled several types of plastic. This village car park had the only decent facilities I'd ever seen in England, and where were they located? In a quiet, practically-deserted car park of a remote village where no-one is likely to find them! Strangely, they didn't have facilities for cardboard, which is commonly recycled.

We headed off with the intention of spending an hour of our remaining time perusing the shops in Matlock Bath, since an hour's free parking was granted along the roadside in town. I was beginning to like Matlock Bath – two free parking spots in one day... This was unreal! However, not long after leaving the car park, we noticed gardens hidden behind a wall and an 'open' sign for Cascades Gardens. We stopped and paid the entry fee, even though it would soon be closed – it was all to raise money for charity, so why not?

We made our way through the entrance and got chatting with the gardener. After explaining that he looked after most of the garden, his conversation took on a life of its own, turning from who-does-what in the garden, to Spain not being the Utopia people thought it was due to freezing winter nights, to Spanish employers not recognising the EU directives, to the lime in the area adversely affecting the local, acid-loving plants, to the geology of Cornwall and Devon, to the high water rates and low wages in the south of England, to the John Major government, and then on to the excesses of Christmas, general commercialism and how similar Christmas was to sex, because it was one big build-up and then it was all over.

Fortunately, that last remark appeared to break the spell of his soliloquy – which was lucky, because I was beginning to wonder whether we'd end up seeing the rest of the garden in the remaining time, even though in actual fact, our information-packed conversation had only taken a surprisingly short time.

Leaving Bonsall, we headed for our next CL site, driving through Matlock Bath, and I spotted a shop sign for the aforementioned Blood Brothers. Apparently, they had their fingers in more than one town pie. Not only were they chimney sweepers but they had a multi-fuel stove business. Could all this really be kosher? Or was it a front for something more nefarious? Steve must have been rolling his eyes towards the sky by now. I'd clearly watched too many Agatha Christie murder mysteries in my youth.

Dethick was another of those places you could drive through without realising you'd done so, and we nearly drove past our CL, despite the directions in the Caravan Club directory.

We settled up on site and, for some reason, I decided to change into my newly-purchased camping clothes. Now, stuck in the middle of nowhere, you wouldn't think you'd need to go through the rigmarole of pulling every single pair of curtains, would you? I mean, unless there's a bird-watcher hidden in the bushes somewhere with his long-range telescope, you're probably safe, right? However, on this occasion, we'd somehow managed to pitch up on the side of the field that was a public right of way and, with walkers passing by at odd intervals, we thought it only polite to spare their delicate British sensibilities.

There was only one other caravan on the site, and the owners popped out (after we'd drawn back the curtains, that is) to say hello and show us where the water tap and chemical disposal were, before returning to their 'van. We've often found this behaviour when campervanning: friendliness whilst leaving you to your own space. I liked that.

In fact, I had always loved my own space in one way or another. Bliss, to me, is looking out from your campervan window at night, seeing barely a streetlamp in the distance and hearing the silence held by the surrounding fields. Yet, without the contrast of everyday life, with its many doings, perhaps I wouldn't appreciate the stillness quite so much.

The next day, we packed up early, made our way back to Matlock Bath and left our 'van in the beloved Pay and Display car park before buying tickets to ascend the steep Heights of Abraham via cable car – although I believe faint-of-heart, vertigo sufferers can reach the Heights on foot.

The weather was warm and clear with blue skies. The views from the Heights took in a wide expanse of the area, and there was enough green space for it not to seem taken over by the sprawling developments below. I thought it would make a great spot for a castle, given its defensive position and regal, minion-surveying outlook. But then I noticed one atop a distant hill and realised my idea wasn't that original after all. With such views, it was almost a shame we'd be underground for a good portion of the morning doing tours.

Woods covered much of the area and after our first tour, we descended the winding, green pathways to wait for our second tour. We sat by the snack shack and watched a group of school kids who had not long finished a tour of their own. They tucked into their nutritious slush puppies before throwing the cardboard containers away.

Now, maybe those recycling facilities back at Bonsall had sparked something off in me, but it got me thinking what a great opportunity was being missed here for educating the kids about recycling – either by their teachers or the cave tour folk. After all, travelling can be one of the most polluting activities, since we tend to buy so many use-once-and-dispose items. But maybe we can at least try to minimise our impact.

All in all, the tours of Rutland and Great Masson Caverns brought to life what it must have been like to be a lead-miner in years gone by, although a bit of creative lighting inevitably pulled us back to modern times. The 'Fossil Factory' would no doubt keep kids occupied for a while, and there was an exhibition mapping out the amazing feat of engineering and construction that lies behind the cable car system. If you're thirsty, pop into the tea shop (it has a steep, leafy view revealing only a hint of the town below) or get the kids to run round the woodland play area a few times, just to make sure they're really tired by the time you get home.

In the wake of my self-righteous gripes at the innocent planet-trashing antics of the school kids, we returned to the camper for a smug, low-environmental-impact lunch in our (not-quite-as-environmentally-friendly) campervan.

After lunch, we thought we'd use our remaining time to explore Matlock Bath. Lovers Walk, leading from the car park, was a winding, tree-lined path overlooking and parallel to the main road of traffic and the Derwent River. The only lovers walking along it seemed to be us – and what a romantic setting it was, with bluebells, pink campions, wild garlic, and the odd cigarette butt, twisted beer can and half-degraded crisp packet to adorn our way!

Eventually, we descended to the river, looping back through the municipal gardens. A relaxing walk had been a nice way of ending our visit to Derbyshire and its caverns.

We were keen to start making our way back down to Cornwall, but we still had time for a stop-off in Staffordshire for a couple of nights along the way. So we fired up the camper, said goodbye to the Pay and Display car park, and headed south…

~ 9 ~
JOURNEY TO THE PAST

We'd done a fair bit of driving by now, and the novelty of doing *The Campervanner's Wave* was wearing a bit thin. It was a code of behaviour we'd adopted from the start, and we'd never really questioned our integrity. I mean, who were we waving to anyway? There are some pretty shonky types around, aren't there? Perhaps we were even one of them!

Maybe this explained why some people waved and some didn't. Had some been travelling so long that they'd seen through the superficial niceties? Or become fatigued, mechanically raising their arms up and down? By the time we arrived at our next destination, we'd made the best of a bad situation by turning it into a game: whenever we could muster the energy to wave, we'd put bets on as to who'd wave back and who wouldn't.

I'd attempted to pre-book a pitch on a campsite on Cannock Chase, a well-known expanse of forest in Staffordshire. The site had showers and it would be convenient for walking out in nature. I sat, goggled-eyed, as I listened on the phone to the booking clerk, who wanted to charge us £48 for two nights – just for the two of us in our Transit-sized campervan. *£24 a night? He must've made a mistake.* Being a polite gent, he was happy to recheck the figures, but it still came out as 'way high' in our estimation – although it did include electric hookup, and he did say it would've been cheaper had we been members of the Camping and Caravanning Club (different again from the Caravan Club).

Surely this couldn't be right – members or not! We could stay in a cheap B&B for that! The only thing I could boil down such a high fee to was simple economics: supply and demand. The area would attract many as the season got busier, and there weren't any other similar sites around. In fact, I'd tried booking CL sites within a reasonable driving distance of Cannock Chase, and several were already full. Yet, even at Three Cliffs Bay in Wales, another sought-after site, we'd only paid £18 per night (albeit in October). Here, they wanted £6 more.

Suffice to say, we ended up rejecting the kind offer to stay at the Cannock Chase site and pitched instead on a Caravan Club CL site a few miles from Lichfield. As we'd booked two nights here (a field with only basic facilities), we'd have to be resourceful and construct a makeshift shower cubicle with an old shower curtain out the back of the camper, heating water for a strip wash. There was no-one around apart from our solitary motorhome neighbours who were parked off at a safe distance. The only other signs of life were the rabbits that popped out from the hedgerows – although they seemed more intent on munching grass than peeking at our briefly-naked rumps.

Despite our willingness to 'rough it' to some extent, the idea of eventually getting a 'van with a shower unit did appeal. After all, there were 'vans around that were only a little longer which housed an on-board shower. Having one would give you an extra degree of freedom, meaning you could stay on basic sites, 'wild camp' or use the 'aires' (free parking places) in Europe. Plus, self-sufficiency would save you money, since you weren't tied to staying on more 'luxurious' sites.

After our 'bush shower', we started tidying up and took a look through the wardrobe. It seemed that our jackets, fleeces (and indeed, Steve's wellies) all took up far too much space: it was full of bulky 'contingency' clothes for every type of weather. What we really needed to be taking away with us, it seemed, were several thinner layers of clothing made of fabrics that dried quickly and stored more easily. Maybe stumbling onto the camping shops back in Bakewell was a blessing after all, and the Hand of Fate had steered us to a solution to a problem we didn't even know we had.

In Bakewell, I had bought two fleece tops and two thinner short-sleeved tops, all made of breathable, light material which 'wicked away' perspiration and was fast-drying. Having two of each item meant I could wear one whilst washing and drying the other. (It also meant I didn't have to choose which colour I liked best.)

Purchasing the short-sleeved tops was serendipitous, as the weather turned out to be even more sunny and sweltering over the next few days, giving me the opportunity to test our their promised features.

There's an old adage that advises never to leave clothes to dry in the room you sleep in. Whenever we'd done so in the confined space of the 'van, it had affected my throat. In any case, washing clothes late in the day normally left us scratching round for overnight drying space indoors if we didn't have drying facilities on our site. So I was glad that my new tops, washed in the warm afternoon before the sun went down, dried in no time and were ready to wear the next day. Their vibrant colours didn't even run in the washing water.

Settling in for the evening, I stared at the mass of travel notes I'd written so far on the trip and was beginning to regret not bringing my computer along for the ride. My aims at packing simply meant I was now in for a long haul of typing everything up when I got home.

The next day was Friday, and we headed off early to Cannock Chase, which my family and I had frequently visited when I was young. Like seeing an old school friend again after decades, certain memories remained, whilst twenty plus years' worth of growth and change without my being around had rendered the treed landscape partially unrecognisable to me. Still, deer populated the protected woods, judging by the numerous 'Deer Aware' signs.

Afterwards, we drove to Fradley Junction, just a few miles outside the cathedral city of Lichfield. We walked along the bank of this busy canal intersection, watching barge folk open and close the locks, then went to the Swan Inn (what my Dad used to call the 'Mucky Duck') for lunch. Inside, we got chatting with some people who had hired a barge for a few weeks. We hadn't realised it was something you could do for a holiday.

In the afternoon, we went to Lichfield, birthplace of Dr Samuel Johnson, most famous for his dictionary of the English language in the 1700s, and also the place I'd grown up in. Although its cathedral makes it a city, I've always thought of Lichfield as a town – something a bit smaller. However, since my last visit (not even a decade ago), it had definitely swollen in size. Now it had extra peripheral roundabouts (to deal with increased traffic) and cloned urban villages and business parks bolted onto the outskirts. Even the medium-sized Tesco supermarket that I once knew had been superseded by one that needed to go on a diet. I wondered if they would have got planning permission to build such an obese store ten or twenty years ago. Times had certainly changed.

As with Cannock Chase, the place now seemed more leafy; and, as we visited my 'old haunts' – St Chad's Church, Minster Pool, the three-spired cathedral, my old home and the town centre, etc – I realised I was actually quite lucky to have grown up there, and especially before it had grown beyond all proportion. Of course, when you're younger, you often don't appreciate things in the same way.

After another night in the area, we planned to dogleg across to visit some of my cousins but, due to unforeseen circumstances, this part of the trip was cancelled. In any case, after our breakfast cuppa, it turned out that we needed to pop back into Lichfield for a new gas bottle. Unlike Bakewell, we weren't spoilt for choice when it came to camping shops. Our predicament made us think it might be a good idea to keep a reserve of gas in store from now on – even if only a lighter, near-empty bottle – just enough for emergencies.

Compulsive tea drinkers like myself might feel conflicted as to whether to use their last dregs of gas to make tea, or to heat water for a shower instead. When faced with such a choice, does one succumb to one's tea-drinking fixation or address one's personal hygiene to spare the sensibilities of the poor sales assistant at the camping shop? For addicts, it's a hard decision. Especially when you consider that such sales assistants are probably used to sweaty trekkers darkening their doorstep, wanting gas for a desperately-needed wash after traipsing about in the blazing British sunshine loaded down with heavy backpacks.

The couple we'd met back at the campsite had regretted not breaking up their long journey up country in two. We therefore decided to stop off at a site halfway down in order to alleviate the stress of driving home in one go. And with our new bottle of gas on board, we set off for the wide expanse of the motorway south, stopping overnight near Burnham-on-Sea, south of Weston-super-Mare...

I never really know what to think of a place whose sign boasts an outdated 'village of the year' award. And Berrow near Burnham-on-Sea, where our next site was located, was one such place.

On the one hand, winning the 'Somerset Village of the Year Award 2004' is indeed a worthy enough claim to fame and showcases the village's standards. (Thumbs up!) However, as the award was granted several years back, it's easy to read the sign as saying: "Yeah, we *had* a quality village a few years ago, but, well, we've let things slip

a bit since then. Can't get another award for love nor money."
(Thumbs down!)

Still, as we pitched up at our site, we realised that we were in no position to judge the village and its standards when our vehicle was in such an unkempt state. It was just as well we hadn't visited my cousins, because the front of the 'van was still shamefully laden with the bodies of dead bugs accumulated the previous weekend on our motorway voyage north. We must've been too busy gadding about to even notice.

Better late than never, we finally faced our Windscreen of Shame square on, with Steve tackling the caked-on cadavers with a soapy sponge and elbow grease. I didn't have the heart to mention we'd probably be sending more to their Maker the next day. At least for now he'd be able to see through the windscreen properly.

The 'van now sparkling, we sat down to polish off the remains of our Bakewell pudding (not tart!) – which we'd intended to share with my cousins – and washed it down with a hot cuppa. Here we were, looking out over a serenely laid-back site. It might have only basic facilities, we thought, but we could only imagine how busy the main centres of holiday tourism would be in this popular seaside area at this time of year.

As we drank our tea, it occurred to us that some motorhomers purposely park next to comparatively cheaper 'vans like ours, just to make themselves look good. On this occasion, we had been stupid enough to pitch up next door to a swish, monster-sized 'van. Although I suppose it could still be considered small by some standards, it was decked out with an all-singing, all-dancing alarm system that would bleep into action every time the owners left their 'van. All at once, we were overwhelmed, envious and awed. But one thing was clear: our neighbours' 'van only served to remind us how relatively poor we were. For, having no alarm system, it was clear we had nothing worth stealing.

Perhaps, I thought, there was an upside to all this. With our neighbours' alarm system waving a red flag to burglars, signalling that they might have something of great value to protect (even if only the pricey 'van itself) maybe they would break into their 'van instead of ours. Yep, perhaps having a cheaper 'van really was better after all.

Not far off, we could see various fowl in an enclosed garden area, although a solitary young Muscovy duck wandered around the site (the only one that really *was* 'free as a bird'), no doubt hoping to do the taste test on our Bakewell. It was getting none of it, and instead I fed it some bread dipped in water. The bird snatched it ravenously from my fingers, squeaking as if desperate in the heat of the day. I held out a glass of water which it guzzled down, all the while wagging its tail with glee. Obviously feeling safe around us (or perhaps just hoping for more food), the duck hung around for quite some time, nibbling at grass seeds and looking into our 'van to check out Steve's bed-making antics.

After watching the duck for a while, I stared it in the face and said, "Hmm, I wonder... If you could talk, what would you tell us, eh?" And, with that, the duck waddled steadily away, obviously psychologically challenged by the remark.

What was it with campsites and birds? Back at Losehill in Derbyshire, I'd seen a couple of ducks. Then there was Henry the pheasant back in Wales. And now a Muscovy duck? Perhaps there was a rumour going round that they were a positive omen for campsites.

At two o'clock the next morning (Sunday), I awoke from slumber and visited the closest thing to a 'ladies' powder room' you can get in a small campervan. How did I know, without looking at my watch, what time it was? Easy! Because the bell of the nearby church rang twice. Why on earth was someone ringing a church bell at this 'ungodly' hour? I wondered. We hadn't heard any ringing earlier that day.

I thought no more about it and went back to bed, but was awake in time to hear the four o'clock chime – which was lucky, as Steve asked if I was awake and would've woken me up anyway. Had I slept through a three o'clock chime?

One could only speculate at what possessed a village to have someone ring the church bell at hourly intervals right through the night. Did they employ someone to sit there all that time? Perhaps they catnapped, setting their alarm to wake them a minute before every hour, so they could be ready to ring the bell on time. Or was there a whole network of bell-ringers working on a shift system so as to spread the burden, each one nominated to ring the bell at a given hour?

Our only other guess at what lay behind the hourly chimes was that it was the work of some insomniac campanologist. Perhaps he was attempting to lull himself to sleep by staying up all night donging an uninspiring monotone chime. If that was the case, it must have done the trick, because we never heard a five, six, seven or eight o'clock chime.

Coming into a Sunday, one would assume the bells would be in full swing to welcome in the morning worshippers. Yet, even as late as eight thirty, we still hadn't heard a sound. Clearly there was a bell-ringing vacancy open for the dawn and daytime shifts! Strange, though, how the obviously-useless night-time ringing had been prioritised over the clearly-more-useful morning toll.

My mind cast back to the Blood Brothers of Matlock Bath, whom my imagination had alleged could be carrying on some nefarious activities under the guise of a normal, plausible façade. Could this be the case here? Was this really a peaceable village community, or was there a shadowy underworld at play here, the bell-ringing being a code to send out signals to some partners-in-crime in a faraway village? By now, only *one* thing was certain: I really *had* watched too many murder mysteries over the years.

Strangely, at nine o'clock, the church bell rang. And it wasn't the melodic flurry of chimes one would expect – it was just a vague attempt at the job. Since there had been no earlier bells, it was feasible that the vicar had turned up to find an empty church. In his panic, he realised he'd have to instigate a Sunday worship 'dong' himself. Determined yet untrained in the ways of campanology, he'd desperately swung on a bell-rope, robes a-flapping, in the hope of drawing in the community flock to prayer. Yet, with the uninspiring tintinnabulation (great word – had to use it!) emanating from the belfry, I couldn't imagine anyone being roused into attending church. In any case, they'd probably be too tired, having been kept awake by hourly chimes throughout the night.

With such a bell-ringing fiasco going on, it was no wonder the place hadn't won another 'village of the year' award – it would only take someone in a competing village to alert the Award Team about these bell-ringing shenanigans, and all future chances at winning would be thwarted.

All things considered, we'd enjoyed our brief stop-over at Berrow and, after breakfast, we left, looping round onto the motorway via the nearby town of Burnham-on-Sea. As it was a Sunday morning, we didn't think it would hurt to park for just a moment on the roadside. But our timing was off. For, the moment I jumped out to take a quick snap across the beach, a bus turned up. The driver looked pretty annoyed, even though his stop wasn't actually where we'd parked. There seemed to be plenty of room for all, but the bus driver was determined to defend his territory – even if it *was* only a few metres long.

This wasn't the first time Steve had made enemies with a bus driver. Back when we'd headed into Lichfield, he'd gotten into the wrong filter lane, unfamiliar with the busy peripheral roads. Both our 'van and a bus waited neck-and-neck at the traffic lights, but we needed to be in the same lane as the bus. So, the second the lights changed, Steve put his foot down, hoping the big bus would be sluggish enough for him to get in front of it. Luckily, the driver wasn't in any apparent hurry, and we managed to switch lanes. Still, we wondered whether we'd ticked the guy off or not; and we drove round thereafter noting any similar buses, wondering if it was the same driver, intent on wreaking revenge on us in some way.

It was lovely to eventually arrive back in Cornwall. Home sweet home!

Still, visiting Lichfield, which had also once been my home, a few things had definitely been stirred up. I'd spent most of my childhood there, then moved away and been quite itinerant for many years, then eventually returned for a time. But I hadn't been back to visit for some years. Why had I gone back, gone over old ground, when I knew nothing stayed the same? What had I been looking for? A sense of what was? A connection to people and place that I might have felt was missing since I left? Had I even realised I might be looking for something by going back?

I still had simple memories of my life back then – like going shopping with my Mum at that Tesco store (or its slimmer version) years ago. Yet it's quite a stark experience to revisit sites whose present reality doesn't match your image of the past. Perhaps it was a sign that I was getting a bit older – although I wasn't sure I favoured nostalgia as a companion. I couldn't remember feeling this way when I returned from five years living in Australia. But things hadn't changed so radically back then – at least, I didn't think so!

It occurred to me that my mother might once have had similar experiences. She came to visit me in 1993 when I lived in Australia. A native herself, she'd lived in Sydney twenty years earlier and it just wasn't the place she knew. My mother had also forgotten the names of native trees she'd always known; and memories of the place in Queensland where she'd grown up didn't match current reality at all. I wonder how I'd feel if I returned to Australia now after such a long time away – all those memories would surely be put to the test.

As we got out of the campervan, however, nostalgia soon took a back seat. I went to check on my tomato seedlings. The weather had been hot while we were away, so it was lucky we'd left them with a neighbour (a former head gardener) to be looked after. Or so I thought! One look in the greenhouse and I couldn't believe my eyes. 'Burnt' wasn't quite the word to describe what I saw. Nearly every tomato plant was frazzled beyond recognition, as if exposed to radioactive material – and we'd only been gone a week!

It was all pretty depressing, but when I went to see our neighbour, he seemed to think he'd done a brilliant job. He was an old fellow, and we knew he was partially-sighted. We just didn't realise things were that bad – and obviously neither did he. He was so pleased at having been able to help out that I didn't have the heart to tell the old boy the truth.

In any case, my advice here is obvious: if you love your plants, make sure they're being looked after by someone who's got 20-20 vision and knows what they're doing... Either that, or just don't go away for more than a few days if the forecast says *HOT-HOT-HOT*.

~ 10 ~
STAR-STRUCK

Steve had already made use of the bike rack fitted onto the back of the camper on our trip to Derbyshire. And, having notched up a number of years as a Cycling Widow, I doubted he'd got a double rack with the thought of whisking me off on romantic holidays where we'd pedal off into the sunset together. No, he was thinking about his forthcoming cycling events and training schedule!

Coming up in June, Steve had a cycle race near Buckfastleigh in the neighbouring county of Devon; and he suggested we plan a trip around it – mixing business with pleasure as it were – by combining his cycling goals with a holiday break away. *Well, why not?* I thought. *No point fighting it.*

By midday on a Friday in mid-June, we were all packed up and ready to go; and, while the heavy holiday traffic pushed its way into Cornwall, we were flying by in the opposite direction, glad to be escaping the 'Silly Season' of tourism that descends upon our home region every year. (If you know which roads to take, of course, you can often escape the holiday traffic. Still, there's no avoiding the ubiquitous tractor or muck-spreader when you take a back-lane short cut!)

By now, we were at the stage where we'd probably wave to the first ten or twenty motorhomes speeding past in the opposite direction, but with so many about at this time of year, the arms soon got tired and the novelty would wear off. So, just a note to anyone reading this who has waved in vain: don't take it to heart – others might not be being snooty, they might just have muscle atrophy from waving at everyone else!

After only an hour and a half's drive, we were at the heart of a whole new holiday experience. Our plan was to visit the famous Burgh Island (set off the south Devonshire coast at Bigbury-on-Sea) before heading north the next day to a site near Buckfastleigh, in readiness for Steve's cycle race on the Sunday morning.

I'd been keen to visit Burgh Island ever since watching Agatha

Christie's *Evil Under the Sun* years ago, since the murder mystery was set and filmed there. The Burgh Island Hotel, built in 1927, eventually fell into disrepair and was apparently restored in the 1980s by a couple of London fashion consultants to its original art deco splendour. However, even the cheapest room at the hotel (the only one on the tiny island) might well be considered to be way out of the league of the average holiday budget. However, since we now had a trusty Autosleeper at our disposal, we could stay on a campsite nearby and visit for free.

The 26-acre tidal island on the 'English Riviera' has acted as a retreat for the rich and famous over the years; and, with any luck, we thought, we might even manage to spot a celebrity or two of our own.

Arriving so early in the afternoon, we decided to head straight to Burgh Island and do some exploring, rather than go to our campervan site. As we neared Bigbury-on-Sea, we were ushered by a Council worker into what was a long and, for the most part, one-car-width country lane, since the main road was being resurfaced. Looking at the map, it might have been considered a short cut, but with the number of cars going through (which some bright spark had omitted to regulate with either workmen or traffic lights) the traffic started backing up pretty quickly in both directions.

Despite all this, everyone involved was surprisingly cooperative, and we managed to sort ourselves out eventually. Such situations make you think twice about what at first appears to be a short cut – especially if you have a bigger motorhome or touring caravan – unless, of course, you actually *like* practising your reverse manoeuvring technique in a tight space!

The 'economy car park' (written in art deco lettering) on the right-hand side before you reach Bigbury beach, is a bit more roomy and works out a bit cheaper than the municipal car park if you are going to be around for more than a few hours – although the latter is right on the beach and handy if you have lots of gear to traipse about.

The low tide at Bigbury-on-Sea meant we'd missed our opportunity to ride on the Sea Tractor: a sturdy, long-legged, four-wheeled contraption which 'ferries' people between island and mainland when the tide's up. Although there was a café on the beach, we were eager to get across to the island while we could, and plumped for a meal at the Pilchard Inn. Although our guidebook had 'promised' soup, baguettes and bar snacks, there was no soup available and, arriving late lunchtime, we were lucky to get a baguette.

We thought we'd wash the baguettes down with a nice, hot brew, but were shocked to discover that they "didn't do tea". Obviously, the writers of our guidebook were no tea-totallers, otherwise they would have warned fellow tea-baggers like us of such a beverage calamity.

"I'll just have water then, thanks," I muttered, no doubt being charged for the privilege. Well, I suppose we *were* on Burgh Island – so what the heck, eh?

Despite the olde worlde charm of the pub's interior, the clement weather invited us to sit outdoors on the pub's picnic tables and watch the world (and hopefully a celebrity) go by as we sat eating our lunch.

"Strange! My baguette's got fig jam in it," I winced. My ever-patient other half gently corrected my uncouth lack of culinary knowledge by pointing out that the 'jam' was in fact chutney, and proceeded to whip a lump of the apparently-offending condiment out of my baguette and place it in his own. "Yummm...!"

"That hotel could do with a lick of paint," I commented, trying to change the subject. We looked about us. Children played merrily on the beach across the way, and a father and son chased each other up and down the length of a large puddle in the sand. It was the stuff of the 'Peter and Jane' books of my youth.

Looking across the coastline, we noticed a beach not far away as the crow flies (what looked like Challaborough on the map) packed with holidaymakers; and I was struck by the sheer numbers in comparison with the quieter beach here at Bigbury.

Our tummies filled, it was time for a long-awaited tour of the island. No celebrities had yet been spotted, either on the beach or in the pub, we remarked. We made our way up the lane and stopped outside the gateway to the Burgh Island Hotel. "Perhaps they do teas in there," I mused, picturing us sipping away as we looked out over the bay from an art deco lounge window. The sign outside, however, announced that it wasn't open to non-residents. *No riff-raff then,* we thought!

Getting onto the designated path which wound its way up towards the top of the island revealed views over the whole area. We could see the hotel's helipad and, over near the tennis courts, what looked like an older, disused helipad, which no doubt doubled as an 'overspill' helipad in an emergency.

Atop the island, said the tourist blurb, there should be a chapel and huer's hut, the latter used as a pilchard lookout post in the old fishing days. However, since all that remained was a sort of stone platform and the ruins of another small building, it was difficult to distinguish which was the chapel and which the hut. I later read that the huer's hut was actually built out of the remains of the chapel, and that the platform was used for military purposes during the war.

As we did a circuit of the island, not only were there stunning open views from every vantage point, but if you have even a passing interest in geology or bird-watching, there would surely be something to engage the eye. According to the hotel's website, numerous rare birds shelter and breed in the area, pods of dolphins and solitary seals frequent the bay, and foxes and badgers play on the higher slopes. Our luck was out: we spotted no marine or land mammals, and the only birds we got a good look at were a gull with its chicks perched cannily on a solitary rock stack near the cliff edge, and a number of cormorants on the crags below at sea level. However, several birds darted about on land, hiding in the bushes as soon as anyone got too close. All in all, the wildlife was proving to be as elusive as the celebrities.

Along the way, we met a Dutch couple who were staying at the hotel. If they'd been hobnobbing with any celebs, they weren't letting on. But in any case, they reckoned they could only afford to stay there one night, what with having to fork out for booze and cigarettes on top of their hotel bill. A likely story! No doubt this was a cover-up for the truth: they were famous Dutch actors trying to escape the national limelight for a few days. But we weren't about to press them on the matter.

Looking down over the hotel as we came to the end of our walk, I had to wonder at past celebrities who had stayed there to escape the world's gaze, and could only guess that they must have felt like prisoners, trapped inside the hotel until high tide, when – like vampires at sundown – they could come out from the shadows and enjoy the delights of the island unhindered by doting admirers.

Again passing the hotel gate on the way down, we saw a couple of 'chancers', the husband trying to persuade the wife that riff-raff really *could* get into the hotel even though they weren't staying there. She held back, unconvinced, as he determinedly dared to push through the gate on the driveway which would lead to the hotel entrance. You had to admire his gumption.

As we walked by the Pilchard Inn on our way off the island, we were brought back down to earth by the pub staff sitting outside on their break (no tea in sight!) discussing the nitty-gritty of work rotas and washing up. We may not have spotted a Dawnus Frenchicus or any Poirot lookalikes, but the beauty of the island and the surrounding coastline were satisfying enough. And, in any case, just what *would* we have said to a celebrity if we'd met one? "Nice day, int it?"

By now, we were desperate for a cuppa and ambled back up the hill to our campervan for a tannin fix.

Suitably quenched, we headed off to our site – this time along the now-chipped, main road. With only a few narrower spots to drive through, we found the roads were surprisingly wide. Despite this, the turn-off to our site, only a few miles from Bigbury, was a bit hairy, with bad visibility in all directions. From the manoeuvrability point of view, we were just glad we had a smaller vehicle.

The owner of our farm site met us at the entrance with a big, genuine smile – in fact, probably the friendliest welcome we've ever had. Although, you never know with country folk. Maybe he'd just inhaled too many manure fumes that day.

Our site at St Anns Chapel was one of the closest to Burgh Island and Bigbury-on-Sea; and our fees gave us access to toilets, showers, electric hookup and country views. There are, however, other sites within easy enough reach, making a nice day trip out from towns like Modbury, Kingsbridge or Salcombe. If you time it right, you can even cut across the estuary from Kingsbridge via a tidal road, thus avoiding the longer trip along the main roads. If you're staying on south Dartmoor for a few days, you could even punctuate your stay with a visit to the coast.

For our evening meal, we cracked open a humble, easy-cook tin of soup each and downed it with slices of bread and butter, but after the light baguette lunch, we still had room for more. Our hunger was in no way quelled by our site neighbours (to our right) unwittingly flaunting their delicious fish and chips supper in front of us, which we couldn't help but notice through their large plush bay-windowed awning.

At odd times, the farm dog would appear from nowhere with a posse of four sheep, acting as if he were trying to earn his keep by rounding them up. None of them seemed at all scared of the mutt, despite their feigned bleats; and the farmer seemed pretty jovial about his enthusiasm despite his lack of sheep-herding skills (the dog's, not the farmer's). It was clear he'd never win any 'One Man and his Dog'-type prizes.

Outside their motorhome, our neighbours (the ones to our left this time) were airing their duvet on a handy little collapsible rotary drier, explaining that they'd been travelling for a few weeks now and their 'van needed a bit of freshening up. They were working their way around England, staying on a site for three days at a time before moving on by about fifteen miles. I dreaded to think how long it would take to complete their tour.

They extolled the tranquillity and spaciousness here, telling us they'd just left another campsite, displeased at the number of 'vans packed in like sardines on a plot the same size as the one we were now on.

The Caravan Club's CLs are limited to taking only five caravans or motorhomes on site, although since our inception into the CL world, we'd noticed a few sites letting in the odd extra one-nighter. We could only guess that the ceiling of five pitches might be imposed by planning law, although no-one seemed to mind so long as they enjoyed their holiday and didn't feel overcrowded.

Invited on a tour of our neighbours' 'van, I couldn't believe how Tardis-like it was. From memory, it was probably six metres in length (seven at most) and inside, there was a spacious bathroom (with shower) and a sizeable worktop in the kitchen. Noticing a flat-screen TV in a wall recess, I asked, "Does it pull out?" The gent grabbed hold of it and swung it out on an arm. "We're watching a film later," he remarked. "We can tilt it round and you can watch it from your campervan next door," he offered, tongue-in-cheek.

As they showed me around, it was clear that, far from being a paragon of simplicity, our neighbours' 'van was seriously geared-up to be a 'home from home'. Their huge fridge-freezer was stocked to weather a third world war and, judging by the electrical items that were plugged in or being recharged (electric bike packs and a couple of mobile phones), they were certainly getting value for money from their site fees. In the average home environment, having so many electricals feeding off the mains goes unnoticed, but not so in the smaller confines of a motorhome.

I mentioned that I'd seen on the CAT (Centre for Alternative Technology) website that you could now get mobile phone chargers which generated power via solar or wind-up. I think I've even seen ones where you can charge a mobile phone as you ride your bicycle – a bit like the old dynamo system for charging bike lights. Although, somehow, I couldn't imagine them winding up rechargeable gadgets while they watched their evening entertainments.

I could well see the attraction of such a plush and spacious motorhome. Yet, with a larger 'van also come drawbacks. Our neighbours found that trying to negotiate smaller roads or car park spots was a hassle. To get around the problem, they often left their 'van on site and used their electric bikes or local buses to get round. Of course, having to recharge bike battery packs means you're tied to sites with electric hookup to a certain extent. And bus ticket prices can often easily compete with Pay and Display fees. Having spent many years commuting in the past myself, I also know that bus routes can sometimes take you off the beaten track, leading you to discover places the tourist literature doesn't tell you about.

I went back to our 'van in awe. I'd never met our neighbours before, and I might never meet them again, but they'd let me into their lives without blinking an eye. It all seemed to be part of this unspoken motorhome fraternity. And yet, perhaps it was more than that.

A few years earlier, when owning a campervan was just a twinkle in our eyes, a dream for the future, we were on holiday in France. We met a French couple on a tour and, when we went back to the car park, we noticed them in their motorhome. Enthusiastic (and perhaps a little cheeky), we knocked on their door to say we liked their 'van. They invited us in without hesitation and we ended up chatting for quite some time. Was it travel itself that opened people up? Or did motorhomers just love meeting people and showing off their 'vans?

Setting the bed up before dark, we watched out the window in amazement as the farmer drove round and round in circles in his tractor in the next field, seemingly without rhyme or reason. His dog was riding shotgun and looked most contented. But what were they up to? When the farmer started doing figure eights, we were really confused. Were they getting in some training for a forthcoming tractor-driving competition? Or was this just the kind of thing that a farmer (and his dog) did for fun on a Friday night round these parts? *Yep!*, I thought, *definitely too many manure fumes!*

As the sun set, orange hues were painted across the open country landscape like the dying embers of a fire. We eventually settled down for the evening, but during the night, I awoke and decided to pop outside for a bit of stargazing.

The fresh night air hit me as I climbed out of the 'van. It was typical country air – not the kind that lets you know 'Farmer Giles' has been about with his muck-spreader, but the wholesome kind that makes your lungs involuntarily fill with volumes of the stuff. Not a peep of traffic could be heard in the distance.

As I looked about and breathed in a deep bellyful of night air, I couldn't help reflecting… We may not have seen any stars on Burgh Island that day but, looking up at the sequined vista, I easily found consolation in the fact that one could not fail to spot a star here!

After a good night's sleep, we got up earlier than normal so I could take some early-morning photos down at Bigbury. Our itinerary for the day was to do a bit of local sight-seeing before heading back up north to stay overnight near Buckfastleigh, where Steve's cycle race was taking place the next morning.

We'd picked up a tip that there was a tidal road short cut which avoided the long drive along the main roads. We took what we thought was the right turning, towards Easton. The road eventually became a steep, seemingly-endless downhill gradient: no doubt we'd need our brakes serviced after this. Were we even going the right way? we wondered. There were no signposts along the way. Finally, we were relieved to reach the bottom. The good news was that there was space to turn at the bottom if the tide hadn't been favourable. The better news was that the tide was low enough for us to drive across.

We made our way to Hope Cove. This was also very downhill (or uphill if you're travelling in the opposite direction); and at the bottom we found a small beach, a small pub, a small café and a small dwelling on a miniature island tenuously attached to the mainland which had clothes drying outside. We could only imagine how the wind must have howled about the place on stormy days. They probably had to nail their washing on the line to dry it.

We just missed out on getting a breakfast at the café, and we didn't fancy burgers and such, so we decided instead to go for a walk along the coast. Our stomachs would have to wait and be fed for the time being on the glorious sunshine and sea vistas.

The views from the coastal path were clear for miles and as we came over the brow of a hill, we could not only see Burgh Island in the distance, but various coves and bays, and what I would refer to as a kind of small Durdle Door (rock archway) in the sea not that far away. As we walked round, a cormorant leisurely held its wings outstretched for a time to dry on the rocks below. Nowhere to rush, nothing otherwise pressing to attend to.

Eventually, our stomachs rang the dinner bell and urged us back to the 'van to cook up a snack. Although our car park had been practically empty on arrival, it was bursting at the seams by early afternoon.

After lunch, we trundled off round the coast in our 'van to St Clements or 'Inner Hope' Cove, following the very hilly roads round the coast, eventually coming to North Sands Bay near Salcombe.

We'd seen adverts in the tourist brochures for what looked like a chirpy, Winking Prawn Café situated on the small beach front at North Sands. There was no way our Autosleeper was going to fit into the 'ample parking' boasted in the café's adverts. Although by no means tiny, the car park was already fairly full, leaving no room for manoeuvre for a larger vehicle. During the main school holiday months soon to come, I'd be surprised if it wasn't heaving, forcing café-goers into yet another cash-harvesting Pay and Display car park next door, thus making a visit to the café that bit more expensive. We hadn't planned on stopping here, but when we headed up the steep climb out of the bay, we chanced upon a free spot of roadside parking, and decided to pop back down the hill to take some snaps of the bay.

An ice cream van stood outside the Winking Prawn Café, complete with its logo of a prawn winking, as if to say it knew something you didn't. However, the van looked like it was now out of commission and only sitting there for show. I wondered whether the prawn logo suggested they might have once sold prawn-flavoured ice cream. If so, had the 'inventive' flavour contributed to the demise of the ice cream side of the business, leaving them to fall back on the café for income? My imagination was piqued.

The café had an inviting menu and, had we not already drunk enough tea to sink a ship, we might well have stopped for a brew and taken in the fresh air and calming views. Instead, we drove round to Salcombe, taking the longer route, as the quicker, coastal road was closed off to larger vehicles.

Parking at the top of Salcombe, we walked into town via back lanes and a small municipal park. The town reminded me of a miniature version of St Ives, with its backstreets and quaint shops, and its pedestrians and car owners all vying for space in the street. Of course, St Ives doesn't have the estuary or yachts of Salcombe, although both towns have their fair share of art outlets awash with mostly maritime works by local painters. It's amazing just how many ways artists find to depict the sea on a canvas.

On the way back to the camper, we noticed a pub with a board outside suggesting women leave their hubbies there while they went off shopping, calling it a 'Men Crèche'. *Great!* So long as they didn't need to wear nappies by the time they left and could drive the car or camper in a straight line!

As we wound our way through the backstreets, we spied a church in Baptist Lane. Thinking it a good photo opportunity, we walked towards it and went round the side of the building where there were some lovely views of the estuary. Everything seemed pretty quiet. And it was only when Steve noticed a number on the door that it dawned on us why there were no congregational cars parked outside: the church had been converted into a residential dwelling! It was then that I caught sight of household items through the porch window; and we made a brisk break for it back to the campervan, feeling rather apologetic to no-one at all.

We knew from our site neighbours back in Bigbury that there was a supermarket and petrol station in Kingsbridge, so we headed off for supplies before driving to our next site some miles away near Buckfastleigh. Despite the usual complaints one often hears about England (such as Pay and Display car parks!), the blessing of having such a small country, is that nearly everything is within short reach.

Our site at Smallcombe Farm, Rattery was another of the Caravan Club's CL sites and, as a recent addition to their list, we'd found it on their website rather than in the Club directory. Not only did we select it because it was close to the start-off point for Steve's cycle race at Buckfastleigh the next morning, but we also wanted electric hookup and shower facilities. After an energetic ten-mile race, Steve would definitely need a good scrub-down.

A delightfully quiet site, we pitched up and were greeted by a herd of cows that had ambled over to the fence-line, curious to meet the new arrivals. There was only one other couple on the site who had been there for eight days – without seeing a soul, they told us.

The site boasted (and delivered) panoramic views over Dartmoor and, waking during the night, I looked out the window to see a clear sky full of stars and again got out to marvel at them. 360-degree views of the sky were unhindered either by streetlamps, tall trees or buildings – no doubt a glorious find of a site for any amateur astronomer. Myself, I can name only a handful of constellations but am nevertheless awed by the night sky, even though the one in England doesn't compare to the sequined night skies I'd seen back in Australia.

I'd heard that a comet was coming close to the earth about this time, and couldn't quite tell if the only likely candidate in the sky was indeed the comet or not. Although you can tell them by their tails, it was just possible that my blurry night-time vision had just given a satellite or star an after-trail instead. Eventually, I went back to bed with only the gentle, hypnotising sounds of the A38 quietly hoovering away in the distance.

The next morning, Steve awoke early to get ready for his cycle race. Had he gone to the event in our normal vehicle, he would have had to get up even earlier to drive all the way to Buckfastleigh, no doubt bleary-eyed, before the event. With the camper, he could sleep in that bit longer and warm his muscles by cycling down the road to the event, arriving relatively fresh-faced and on form with a better possibility of riding a decent race.

Having said that, my status as a long-suffering Cycling Widow was further reinforced by Steve's clattering about whilst getting ready – all inches from my head as I attempted to return to the Land of Nod. *Hmm... Holiday, indeed,* I thought.

After a few more clatter-bang-clunks inside and outside the 'van – all magnified and echoed by the stillness of a Sunday morning in the countryside – I managed to snooze briefly before being pulled back out of my enjoyable state by Steve whispering "I'm off now" and clicking the door firmly shut. *Thanks a bunch! No chance of me getting back to sleep now!*

When the site owner came round later to collect our fees, it turned out that they hadn't quite put the finishing touches to the shower facilities in time for their first intake, but the owner was kind enough to let us use his home shower instead.

It turned out to be a beautiful day and, as I tidied away the bed, the farm dog came round the 'van, eventually settling by the back door. She looked a bit desperate for company, because even after giving her some attention, she hung round the 'van as if waiting for more. I later saw that she'd moved her allegiances and was hanging round another motorhome door, hoping someone else would come out and give her a scratch or two.

Steve returned from his race and, like a ball on a piece of elastic, the dog shot back across as soon as she saw him. After having a bit of attention (the dog, not Steve), he went for a shower and we sat down to lunch and reviewed our holiday. The bike rack had turned out to be quite useful again, and the only drawback seemed to be that the bars extended almost a full 'van width, so you had to allow for that when going in and out. And, despite the noisy early-morning palaver, Steve's cycling event had been a good excuse for a weekend trip in the campervan. We'd seen and done a lot in such a short space of time. Had we gone to Bigbury and Buckfastleigh on separate trips, we would also have guzzled more fuel.

All in all, although Bigbury was a dogleg off the main route, it was still an economical way of working things. And Steve would be doing other races here, so we could look forward to a few more mini adventures over this side of Devon in the future...

~ 11 ~
THE MAGIC OF CORNWALL

It has to be said that, given the choice, we'd holiday in the quieter mid or low season. However, for many, it's not always possible to do so; and if you have children, your options are often limited to the British summer school holidays in July and August. On the plus side, there's a higher probability of getting some decent weather. However, on the down side, sites are at a premium and you'll often be joining a league of other holidaymakers all jostling for position on the congested motorways, teeming beaches and overcrowded tourist attractions.

My sister was planning a trip down to Cornwall with her son in July, planning to stay near my parents' place in Newquay. A busy resort on the west coast of Cornwall, the town is popular with surfers, families wanting a bucket-and-spade holiday, and those who love the nightlife and clubs. And, although we don't live that far from Newquay ourselves, we decided to make a holiday of it and booked ourselves in for a night on a site at Mawgan Porth, a few miles north of Newquay.

Magic Cove, an independent site (not the Caravan Club this time), had been recommended to us by some neighbours who'd stayed there once or twice in their caravan. They'd been enchanted by the place, which is only a short walk from the beach and cafés.

At this time of year, the site was packed and the pitches therefore quite cosy. No doubt we'd been spoilt by our stays on more spacious CL sites. The site seemed quite organised and when we arrived, after reception had closed for the day, a sign told us which pitch to take. The toilet block was also spick and span.

Normally when we went away, we weren't bothered about mobile phone reception. However, wanting to make plans to meet up with my sister the next day, I had to walk back and forth between beach and site to try and get a network signal and to check my messages. We later read in the site leaflet that there was free wifi internet on site, so anyone with the right device could probably get in touch via email or other apps like Skype or Messenger instead.

The next day, the weather was beautiful and we met my sister et al for a late breakfast. Our café overlooked the beach and the food was tasty. The main coastal road was nearby, so it was handy that there was a garden area for my nephew to play in while we ate.

Magic Cove is away from the main holiday crowds in Newquay, yet handy for all sorts of activities like surfing, golf, cycling and walking. Parents could just as easily spend a day at the beach with their kids – and all within a few minutes of the site.

Our neighbours had clearly enjoyed their holiday on the site (not sure what time of year it was). However, given that we already lived within driving distance of Newquay (albeit in a different direction), I don't think we benefited overall from staying on the site for just one night. Not only did I have trouble contacting my sister, but we had to vacate our pitch by 11am the next morning, leaving us to scratch round for somewhere to park the 'van while we had brunch.

Still, our time there certainly wasn't wasted and, if you don't try things, you never know...

~ 12 ~
DIPPING INTO DEVON

Steve had another cycle race at Buckfastleigh in Devon at the start of August, giving us another excuse for a weekend break away. As with our last visit there, we'd spend a night at Bigbury near Burgh Island then head back up to Buckfastleigh.

Not only did mizzle (Cornish for 'misty drizzle') fill the roads on our departure day, but so did tailbacks. And since we normally avoided 'Silly Season' travel, we didn't know if there'd been an accident or if a couple of bored tractor drivers (no doubt high on manure fumes) had decided to have a laugh by commandeering both lanes further up the highway.

Nearing our destination, we looked out towards the sea, which was shrouded in mist. No doubt it would be a write-off for taking any photographs. However, it was now four o'clock and, having spent two hours glued to the campervan seats already, we weren't going to pitch up on site and spend the next couple of hours trapped in our 'van staring at the rain. We needed to stretch our legs, whatever the weather.

On a whim, we took a detour, following a sign towards Challaborough. On our last trip, walking round Burgh Island, we'd seen a beach full of holidaymakers at what looked like Challaborough, whilst Bigbury-on-Sea seemed empty in contrast.

We went through Ringmore village and, instead of heading for Challaborough (the road downhill looked too narrow for our liking) we settled in the National Trust car park above Ayrmer Cove.

In contrast to our normal aversion to Pay and Display car parks, we didn't begrudge a donation towards the car park fees here, which funded hedge-laying, path-clearing and other work that the National Trust do. This keeps paths open for visitors like us who want to enjoy the beauty of such areas without having to fight through vegetation like an explorer in the Amazon jungle.

After a decent walk downhill, we neared Ayrmer Cove and, surprisingly, the mist had cleared, opening the view enough to reveal a section of the beautiful south coast cliffs: vertical, steely-grey strata that would once have been horizontal layers of sediment.

We walked up onto the bluff. It was low tide and, from this angle, you could see Burgh Island in the distance as well as the sandy stretch connecting island with mainland. Not for the first time had we chanced the weather and ended up with it clearing to reveal some stunning views.

One thing that really struck us was that there was hardly a soul around. It was early August – peak holiday season in England – so how come it was so quiet? Back in Cornwall, you could visit places like Port Isaac or St Ives and they'd be heaving with tourists. Having said that, if you knew where to go, you could usually find a quieter spot not that far away.

We'd met other travellers who'd noticed the same thing: that people often flocked to the same spots. If you're a family wanting to be in the thick of things, then you'd obviously be wise to head off to those spots. After all, if you have kids, it's often nice to holiday with others around so they have some playmates. But if you prefer it otherwise, then it's nice to know you can dodge the crowds, too.

By the time we'd driven to Bigbury, it was getting on for six o'clock, and a fish and chips supper from the local shop sounded most appetising, freeing us from the evening washing-up chores whilst providing a welcoming hot meal. Last time we'd stayed on site here, we'd dined on tinned soup and bread, only to be 'upstaged' by neighbouring holidaymakers eating fish and chips in the comfort of their large awning while we just looked across and drooled. It wasn't going to happen again! This time we were thinking ahead!

Settling on our site at St Anns Chapel near Bigbury, we chomped away on our fish and chips (hoping for a few envious looks), watching children play football and chase each other round the site field. It was quite a different picture from our last visit here. A few months back, there had mostly been what looked like older or retired couples, some with their little dogs in tow. This time, there were also younger adults with children. Even so, being a CL site, it was still a world away from the bigger sites which seem to attract a more lively crowd.

The evening was relaxing, watching the children potter about in the background. Three 'vans' worth of people looked like they might have come together, since they were all packing up their awnings while it was dry and helping each other out in the process.

The weather was changeable in the night, with rain lashing down intermittently onto the 'van, but by morning the three 'vans and accompanying cars were gone, having made no sound in the process of leaving.

Making do in our little camper, we were intrigued as to the fact that people pull up with a large caravan, trailer tent or motorhome – which looks more than spacious enough to holiday in – then go to the trouble of erecting an awning.

In essence, I can't help feeling that awnings are just like tents, engendering the same problems. And, having camped in tents ourselves some years back, we were slightly averse to such contraptions. Given that the British weather is so unpredictable, you never know if you're going to get rained out or be living for a week caught in gale-force winds. And if your tent is wet when you pack it away, you still ideally have to dry and clean it at some point soon after. In a hot country, it might be a different thing, but Britain doesn't exactly appeal to me as a camping destination.

If unending sunshine is miraculously forecast for your holiday or you have kids, I could see that an awning might be worth the trouble of putting up. Still, lots of people enjoy them whatever the weather, and they clearly give you a feeling of spaciousness as well as an extra 'room' to chuck things like muddy or sandy shoes (thus avoiding a mucky 'van) and provide a sheltered spot to sit in of an evening as you watch the sun go down. And, let's face it, if we'd had an awning, we could've sat there, eating our fish and chips, whilst our site neighbours drooled at us through luxurious plastic windows, wondering where on earth we'd bought them from.

In view of the blustery weather and intermittent rain, we had a nice, lazy morning in bed the next day, watched over by two female cows and babes in the neighbouring field. A programme was due on the radio that we fancied listening to over lunch, so Steve popped to the village shop while I cleared away the bed. The shop being no more than two minutes away on foot, Steve should have been back well in time to help prepare our meal before the programme began. But where was he? I wondered, as I finished tidying up. Visions of him being mown down into the hedgerow by a speeding tractor or hapless caravan-towing holidaymaker flashed through my mind.

No sooner had the thoughts appeared than Steve turned up, safe and sound, just in time for the radio show, but not before spouting on about his chat with the local store owner who'd recently contended in an Ironman event in Switzerland. It's amazing just who you can end up meeting in a village shop in the middle of 'nowhere'!

After lunch, we wound our way on towards our next site, stopping off in what looked like a quaint little town. We browsed an organicy-type food shop before ducking into a small supermarket-cum-convenience store for groceries. The moment we put a discounted, shrink-wrapped broccoli on the counter with our other goods, we were asking for trouble! As the checkout girl swiped the barcode, it appeared that the item was 'out of date' and that we couldn't buy it.

Now, I don't know if I'm just getting more belligerent as I get older, but I suddenly got the urge to heartily defend the rights of this perfectly good broccoli to be sold and given a good home. The shop assistant wasn't going to budge, so I asked if we could kindly see the manager. She arrived, and we argued the merits of product labelling and the difference between 'best before' versus 'use by' (no doubt to the consternation of the people behind us in the queue), but the manageress wasn't going to budge any more than the checkout assistant. She obviously thought it was more than her job was worth to sell us this firm, green broccoli – which bore no hint of deterioration (OK, maybe because it was laminated in shrink-wrap) – even though it probably shouldn't have still been on the shelf.

We'd clearly reached stalemate and, with no more broccoli available on the shelf, (to the relief of the other customers) we took our custom back to the health food-type store and bought a non-plasticised broccoli at double the price. Oh, well, it *was* organic!

Over our evening meal, I reflected upon the day's events. Did my attitude have any positive effect on the manageress? I didn't think so. As I sat at the table, chomping away on my tasty, organic broccoli, I pictured her getting home from a hard day's work, bemoaning the number of vexing customers she'd had to deal with that day to her husband.

"Anyway, love, I've brought us a few freebies home for dinner," I'd hear her say in my imaginary scenario. "Some meatballs, a nice green broccoli, and a lovely pudding for afters. Nothing wrong with them, as usual – they're only a day past their 'best before' date, but I'm not allowed to sell 'em, see. Couldn't let them go in the dumpster, though, could I?"

We settled in to bed that night, and I could only pray that I wouldn't be tossing and turning all night, having nightmares about some broccoli I'd apparently been swizzed out of. Perhaps it had gone to a good home after all – just not ours!

The last time we'd stayed on the CL site at Rattery near Buckfastleigh, Steve had managed to make quite a racket getting ready for his early-morning bicycle race, clunking and clattering just about everything in the 'van, inches from my head. This time, he'd got everything prepped the night before, in the hope of making as little sound as possible and seamlessly slipping away to the race meet-up point. Well, that was the plan, anyway.

As I lay there trying to get back to sleep after the alarm rang, I could hear a sound outside the 'van, like a distant buzzing. Just what were the odds of a bee passing by our very 'van at this hour just as Steve was spreading honey onto his bread? I wondered. The bee must have been a flippin' insomniac! Or maybe it was returning home from a night out, having had one too many slurps of nectar.

Steve pulled down the skylight to bar entry, but then the persistent little creature started bouncing around outside the back of the 'van as if to work its way in through the crack between the doors. But, eventually, it realised it was a lost cause and gave up the ghost.

By now, it was clear I wasn't going to get any more sleep, so I decided to see Steve off at the farm gate. Despite his attempts at being quiet, the stillness of the morning only served to magnify the click-click-click of his bike's freewheel as we walked along the fence-line, accompanied by the ever-curious cows in the neighbouring field.

What a sight we must have made: Steve in his Smurf-like cycling gear and me looking like a dishevelled bag-lady in my pyjamas. The scene would have looked strange enough to humans, if any of them had been insane enough to be up at such an unearthly hour on a Sunday morning, but what must it have looked like to the cows? There was nothing (that I knew of, at least) that equated to a bike in the bovine world.

As I kissed Steve goodbye, he managed to top his earlier noise-making by catching his bike pedals on the farm gate's metal bars. If he hadn't woken our motorhome neighbours before, he surely would now. It sounded like someone ringing a dinner gong. Seemingly oblivious, he snapped his cycling shoes loudly into his pedals before pushing off. As he did so, the gate swung noisily around and I thankfully caught it before it hit the fence-post and sent resounding shockwaves to every 'van on the site.

Sitting with a hot cup of tea back at the camper, I opened the curtains and watched as the mist gradually gave way to sunshine. The cows drifted in rhythm with the clouds, peacefully munching on grass, with the Dartmoor hills as their backdrop. Did they ever marvel at the views? I wondered.

Since our last visit, the shower in the toilet block had been fixed and I noticed the owner had not only left his tourist pack there for visitors to borrow, but he'd also put in recycling facilities for everything normally collected from residential areas.

Full-facility Caravan Club sites all seem to have a washing-up room as standard, but with CLs such as this, you often have to fall back on your own washing-up bowl and kettle. The sink at our site might accommodate a few cups and small bowls, but it wasn't cut out for a full meal's dishes.

If you were camping in a tent, the home comforts of a full-facility site – like hot water and plenty of space to wash up in – wouldn't go amiss, but since we had facilities in our own camper, we much preferred staying on a quieter site where the views consisted of green space, rather than rows of white metal boxes on wheels.

After washing the breakfast dishes, I sat outside in my deckchair to write. Chamomile wafted on the air – the little yellow and white flowers were everywhere if you looked. The farm dog (who we later found out was called Rosie) appeared. I remembered how hungry she'd been for attention the last time we'd stayed there. If you stroked her as much as she seemed to want, she'd probably be bald. Now that I was outside the 'van, she didn't seem to want to leave, so it was lucky that, when the site owner came to collect our fees, she velcroed herself to him instead, leaving me to do a bit of writing before Steve returned.

Had Steve consulted the five-day forecast at the start of the week, he might have decided not to race, for the outlook was rain, rain and more rain. As the week progressed, however, the forecast miraculously changed, to predict 'sunny intervals' for Sunday, the day of the race. In fact, we had 'all sunshine and no intervals' instead, and the wind was calm enough to get a good race in.

On the way back home, we decided to find somewhere to park for a late lunch. I noticed a sign on the map marking some kind of green or forest area, and we turned off to find it. In the absence of signage, we more or less had to follow our noses and, having driven through a few estates, eventually struck gold.

By now, our energy was flagging. We luckily got the last remaining parking space at the roadside beneath the forest canopy, and whipped up some spaghetti on toast and a hot cuppa.

What a lovely, tranquil space, we marvelled just before a bunch of kids walked by the 'van, laughing loudly and shouting.

It turned out that Plymbridge Woods was a popular spot, tucked away yet within easy reach of Plymouth. Several people wandered by either in groups or with dogs; and the odd car drove past, realised it just couldn't squeeze in, and moved on. No doubt the residents of the local estates found the green spot a welcome relief from the trappings of grey suburbia.

After lunch, we went for a walk to stretch our legs. We could hear a lot of noise some distance away in the forest. The path eventually opened up to reveal a creek – and the source of the sound: a family playing in the water. It was surprising how much the voices of so few had been magnified by the forest.

Eventually, we turned tail and headed home. We were tired after unpacking and were grateful for having bought an oven meal at the supermarket when we stopped for fuel.

A week later, Steve had another cycle race. We decided to drive the camper up there for just one night, staying again at Rattery, although this time, we didn't try fitting in any other sight-seeing.

Steve was so happy to have shaved a whole five minutes off his PB time (Personal Best) that, in his excitement, he left his tool kit and other bits behind at Cycling HQ in Buckfastleigh after the race.

As we drove into Buckfastleigh to retrieve his belongings, I noticed the sign describing the town as an 'Ancient Woollen Town'. Now, to me, that doesn't instil confidence. It conjures up images of infirm, indecisive, 'woolly' townsfolk… or of fluffy old cartoonified buildings and people, all made of wool. On the plus side, however, it probably means the community knits together well! (Sorry!)

This was Steve's last race of the year in this area, and we'd really enjoyed having a few brief breaks. It's not only amazing how much you can do staying away for a few nights in your camper, but how time seems to expand when you change location and do something different.

Because we'd been to these same venues and sites a few months earlier – and therefore ticked off certain places we'd wanted to see – it was nice to just go away and not have too major an itinerary, stopping off at previously-uninvestigated places at will.

Half the fun of being on holiday is being able to slow down, relax and amble along like a 'Sunday driver' – no matter what day of the week it is... So it's not unknown for us to occasionally trundle along at a merry 40mph.

Trouble is, one man's relaxation is another person's stress. And, living in a popular tourist destination ourselves, we have to remember how annoying it can be getting stuck behind a holiday-making Sunday driver when you're trying to get somewhere! In our area of Cornwall, 30mph is about the favoured speed of a holidaymaker on a country road, where you stand not the slightest chance of ever overtaking them, even when they slow down to 20mph on the bends. In any case, while I'm on the subject, I'd like to posit that, whoever thought of putting National Speed Limit signs on country lanes must have been having a laugh. Who but a boy racer or Scrumpy-fuelled tractor driver would ever dream of trying to go 60mph on a narrow, snaking, one-lane road?

Still, as we drove home, it was clear we were in danger of becoming an annoying slowcoach on a fast road! *Either that, or we were attracting a fan base or convoy*, I thought, looking out the back window. Having one or two vehicles behind us is one thing, but a tailback is just plain embarrassing. As the cars made a desperate bid to overtake us, no doubt seething at our leisurely gait, we were fortunate on this occasion to be able to transfer their wrath from us onto the snail-like tractor in front of us.

When stuck behind a farm vehicle (as the folk who overtook us were), you might like to bear in mind a statistic I read in a motorhome magazine that said something to the effect that tractors will only ever be travelling between about one and three miles before turning off into a field. Still, I guess if it's travelling at 5mph, you'll still be trailing behind for quite a while. And how anyone works these figures out – or who would want to go to the trouble of doing so in the first place (and why) – is beyond me.

Anyway, here's a parting thought to ponder: Have you ever wondered at how we rush about so much most of the time, then get so exhausted from it all that we need a holiday just so we can slow down...?

~ 13 ~
MODERN WHEELS & ANCIENT STONES

After the summer 'Silly Season' comes what I think of as 'Straggler Season' – that time of year when school children in England are just going back to school, and when there are a still a few 'stragglers' on the roads trying to get in a holiday before the colder autumn weather well and truly sets in.

It's often also around this time that campsites get a little less populated and reduce their fees to low-season tariffs. So there's still a bargain to be had – and one with fewer holidaymakers vying for a pitch. Excellent for retirees or for folk like us who have no children and would like to think they've retired early.

We had a week free to do as we pleased, so we pre-planned a visit to the early-September motorhome show in Shepton Mallet, Somerset, followed by a few days at my sister's place in Bristol, before looping back towards the standing-stone sites of Avebury and Stonehenge in Wiltshire.

We worked out a rough route the week before leaving and I bought tickets to the motorhome show and pre-booked sites. This would save us looking for a site after a full day's sight-seeing and save on fuel because we weren't meandering about so much. We also hadn't bothered looking up the forecast for this trip as the weather had been so changeable lately; and we opted instead to take clothes to suit all weathers.

Despite setting off in good time at midday, a five-mile tailback on the A30 had us crawling along at 5mph beneath an overcast sky. It wasn't the first time we'd had an opportunity to enjoy watching the cows in the roadside fields chomping lazily on grass while the world rushed by in their cars trying desperately to get somewhere. In other fields, rolls of hay lay dormant like golden bobbins.

Whenever I'm caught in traffic, I can't help wondering just where all my fellow travellers are going. To some all-important hair appointment? To deliver happiness to someone in the form of a gift package? Or sadness in the form a court summons? *Only 1.5 miles tailback remaining*, promised an electronic highway sign, as we suddenly sped up to a dizzying 10mph.

For a while, we were stuck behind a dairy truck. For some reason, the driver kept jamming his brakes on. If he kept that up, we thought, he'd have a wagon full of cream by the time he arrived at his destination.

It dawned on us as we headed north, that this was not only our last longer trip of the year, but also the culmination of our year's experiment in owning a campervan. *Crikey, was it only a year ago that we'd bought our campervan?* Me, out of sheer restlessness and Steve, perhaps partly to shut me up.

Ironically, Steve had been the one who had not only got right into the technical side of campervans, but had delved deeper and inadvertently got hooked – to the extent where I was now getting a running commentary on nearly every campervan that went past. *Oh, joy! If only I'd known what I was starting!* I thought. Sometimes, I had to worry whether Steve's eyes were in fact on the road or ogling the campervan eye-candy passing by. If he leched after other women like he did motorhomes (or indeed his beloved bicycles), I would have left him long ago!

Finally, the traffic thinned out and cars shot by like corks held too long in a fizzy champagne bottle. Soon we were moving onto the M5 at Exeter. The road sliced through the hillside exposing the beautiful iron-rich, rust-coloured earth, famous on Devon's 'Jurassic Coast'. Despite our tendency to trundle along at a heady 55 to 60mph on the motorway, we managed to arrive at my sister's in Bristol at a respectable at 5pm.

Just before we went away, we discovered problems with the electrics; and we couldn't pinpoint whether it was a fault with the leisure battery or the general electrics of the 'van. Either way, we didn't have time to sort it out before leaving so we'd just have to do without indoor lighting. No doubt we'd have to spend a wedge of cash on having what was probably a small problem looked at when we got back – or else we'd have to bribe a fourteen-year-old electronics geek with chocolate bars and crisps into fixing it.

What we hadn't figured on in all this was the knock-on effect with the fridge. Although it could run on gas, it needed a spark of electricity to ignite the flame. Had we realised this earlier, we could have booked sites with electricity. As it was, we wouldn't be on a site with mains hookup till mid-week. But, camping outside my sister's for a few days, we could at least pop stuff in her fridge or freeze cool-blocks to keep the temperature down in our own.

On the plus side, the seasonal weather was unlikely to deliver a heatwave, so we could still use the fridge for food storage, taking care with things like milk and cheese. On the down side, the nights were drawing in; and we'd found out through previous experience that, whilst you could just about manage with torches in a small space come evening, setting up our bed was best done early with the help of natural light.

We were also glad to find that the container of toilet fluid that came with the 'van had finally run out. Personally, I wasn't too keen on the chemicals used in these porta-loos. Not only from an environmental standpoint, but also because they were pretty strong-smelling. The fluid we'd inherited with the 'van was probably a major brand, but within the confines of the campervan, it stripped the lining off the back of your throat. Or had we just not diluted it enough? In any case, we refilled the toilet's fluid compartment with a new, non-toxic, 'green' brand, breathed a whole lot easier as a result – and it still seemed to do the job (sorry – truly no pun intended!).

This wasn't the first time we'd slept in the 'van outside my sister's place in Bristol. Despite her living just off a main road, it had been surprisingly quiet on our last visit – even to the point of rivalling a site in the country. Not this time, however. Parked at the end of the small cul-de-sac, there were many more comings and goings through the night. But luckily, I always travel with my earplugs and eye-patches. You never know when you'll need them. And, although they don't block out all noise and light, they do help blot out the worst of what would otherwise make for a bad night's sleep.

The next day we drove to the Royal Somerset and West Showground in Shepton Mallet in my sister's car with tickets in hand to see the Motorhome and US RV Show. This would be our first-ever visit to one of these events; and a bit of research showed there are several held in England throughout the year, with a major show at the NEC (National Exhibition Centre) in Birmingham, right in the heart of the country, central for UK visitors, with lots of parking (over 20,000 places, in fact).

Buying tickets for my sister, her husband, their little son and ourselves before the event worked out cheaper. And, although the show ran for the whole weekend, with entertainments and the possibility of booking a pitch on site, we decided a day visit would do for starters.

Looking across from the top of the hill car park, it didn't look like there was much going on, but once you crossed the entrance threshold, the beginnings of a much larger event became visible; and judging by the site plan, there was lots to see and do. With plenty of parking, and attendants decked out in regulation hi-viz tops, the show looked well organised from the start. Even the Tardis-lookalike porta-loos and main toilet block were clean – not the stinky, blocked-up affairs one might expect at big events. At least, they weren't at this early juncture.

A section near the entrance was allocated to motorhome pitches, rented out for the duration of the show. One 'van had several bricks under its wheels to bolster it up. How they mounted the 'van onto that precarious height of bricks in the first place – or why anyone would prefer to lug several bricks around in their 'van – remains a mystery. It was all rather makeshift and, whilst 'Waste not, want not' is a noble enough motto, when the bricks are subsiding under the weight of the vehicle, you know it's time to invest in some proper levellers.

The first real sign of the show was a semi-circle of 'vans displayed for sale and, being motorhome show newbies, we entered the first 'van with childlike enthusiasm. As we tested the springiness of the lounge seats, I wasn't sure who was the biggest kid in our troop: Steve, or my little nephew!

Even though we weren't imminently going to buy a new 'van, Steve always seemed to be dreaming about a next 'van and would constantly be on the lookout wherever we went. Since he's also been an avid cyclist for a long time, I'd got used to this kind of behaviour: ever the 'roving eye' for the next best mechanical contraption.

Having checked out 'vans on the internet for the past year or so (more out of interest than necessity), we were keen to get a feel for the external size and inner space of various 'vans. It's one thing to check them out in a picture (many websites have inside shots of 'vans) but wide-angle lenses have a habit of transforming cupboardy nooks into spacious palaces.

As Steve always seemed to have his head in either a cycling or motorhome magazine, he'd managed to absorb what I thought of as the 'intricacies' of the campervan world. Understanding the difference between 'coach built' and 'van conversions' might be simple enough, but the details still sieved out of my brain like sand through an egg-timer not long after taking the information in. Steve, on the other hand, is a natural with that sort of thing.

Apparently, if you take the front and base of a van, then add a fibre-glass shell (plus insides), you call it a 'coach built'. Conversely, if the outer (metal) van is retained, and only the insides converted to a particular design, what you have is a 'van conversion'. So, even if you don't remember the difference between the two types, it seems to me that the most important thing to know is whether the main body of the vehicle is liable to rust, since this means more upkeep and expense.

Some motorhomes come with fixed beds, saving time (and your back muscles) setting them up at night. Rock-and-roll style beds are often found in certain 'vans, like VWs, and as mentioned earlier in the book, these pull out quickly and easily, although they do hamper access to some of the cupboards. For every 'give', there's often a 'take' when it comes to motorhomes.

Many 'vans are similar to ours in that the beds can be arranged in a number of ways, depending on your needs. For a quick setup, you can have two singles (one on each side of the camper), or there's the more time-consuming double setup. If you're not too tall, you might be able to get away with sleeping transversely (with your head and feet pointing toward the sides of the 'van). However, Steve found this setup too restrictive in our 'van, so we have to lower the front seats to make up the bottom part of a lengthier bed. This isn't usually necessary in longer 'vans, and thus leaves the driving seats accessible.

It became clear, as we moved on, that the show was going to be one massive sweetshop of 'vans – new and second-hand ones, big rigs and compact campers – as well as a harbour for any and all motorhome accessories and services: electric bikes, micro-fibre cleaning cloths, holiday 'van hire, memory foam, upholstery outfits, tour planning – you name it.

The atmosphere was fairly relaxed and, despite the amount of people milling about, it was still possible to view the inside of most 'vans without too much 'competition' from fellow rubber-neckers.

Only a few stalls were packed out. One displayed three well-designed campervans which you could hire on a try-before-you-buy basis – a low-risk way of finding out if you really wanted to fork out £36-plus grand to own one (minus half of the hire fee, of course!).

Another 'honeypot' that had folk buzzing round like bees displayed a large, swish, all-singing, all-dancing motorhome. You could practically stand up in the rear storage area, and the lounge and kitchen were so packed that I thought there was a party going on in there. I moved on. The highly-veneered £140k rig really didn't impress me! Far too awkward to drive and park up. *Anyway, I'll take my comparatively cooped-up, ageing Transit any day, thanks*, I thought.

To my nephew, the show was like one big playground; and he was so enthusiastic about one vehicle that he somehow slipped away unnoticed to the front cabin and gave the horn a loud honk. I'm not sure what the stall owners thought, but we weren't going to hang around long enough to find out.

Caught up in the vortex of enthusiasm no doubt generated by such events, I suspect the motorhomes on offer would be rather seductive, even for those who weren't previously planning on buying a vehicle.

I have to admit here that we were indeed tempted to buy a slightly bigger campervan ourselves, but held off. The vehicle in question was another Autosleeper – a newer, Symphony model similar to our own. Although we managed fine with ours, a slightly longer 'van like this one would still be easy to manoeuvre and we'd get a washroom with shower and toilet for the extra metre in length. It even had a quick-setup bed. However, paying ten thousand pounds for the privilege of a few extras did put us off slightly. There were also a lot of nice Autocruise designs that had similar facilities, although these 'vans were a little bigger.

Whereas I wouldn't necessarily want to dissuade anyone from buying a 'van at one of these shows, it's certainly worth taking at least a small step back from the temptation to impulse-buy, asking yourself a few questions before you fork out your hard-earned (I've listed some suggestions in a handy section at the end of the book).

Probably, the more you think through such things before you buy, the happier you'll be with your 'van. Having said that, we didn't think things through that thoroughly ourselves and were thankfully all right – although it might have been a more foolish purchase had it been a more expensive 'van.

In any case, owning a motorhome seems to be a work-in-progress. Buy a 'van, try it out for a while, and it'll reflect back to you what you'll need in your next 'van. However, be aware that reselling a brand new 'van after only a short while will lose you money. Good news, of course, for those of us who are quite happy with tried-and-tested second-hand 'vans.

After only a few hours, we'd seen lots, but we hadn't managed to see everything – no doubt why they hold these events over three days. We hadn't even touched on the US RV (American Recreational Vehicle) part of the show, although we'd visited a local RV sales outlet in Cornwall (Itchy Feet) some time back out of curiosity.

RVing truly is another world again from your average motorhome. When we turned up at Itchy Feet, we were amazed at the multitude of vehicles parked up. Some even had side panels that opened out to create full-sized lounges and bedrooms once on site, making the rigs a true 'home from home'.

Having subscribed to an RV newsletter in America, I learnt that quite a lot of people buy RVs either to live in or to travel in part of the year. Go online and you can see all manner of videos about people living out of these giant rigs, especially in America and Australia, where there is plenty of space and a network of open roads. However, certainly in towns and cities at least, it looks like some have been clamped down on for living in a motorhome on the streets. Possibly, they'd get away with it out in the sticks. But, if you wanted to work at a fixed place for any length of time in the town or city, it might be a problem.

A few years back, I heard that the Walmart supermarket chain in America allows motorhomers to stay overnight in their car parks. No doubt, they benefit from holidaymakers spending money in store and on the forecourt. However, an incident occurred some time ago, in which a man forcing his way into a motorhome was shot by the owner. Obviously, this brings up issues of security and liability, but I understand many of their stores (though not all) still permit overnight stays.

In England, I heard a rumour that the UK's Tesco supermarket was also friendly towards overnight campervanners (allegedly because some head honcho at Tesco was a motorhome owner). In any case, not only does the aforementioned honcho no longer seem to be a 'head', but this was only hearsay and I'd definitely advise motorhomers to check a supermarket's policy first before parking willy-nilly in their parking lot – especially as the UK supermarkets in general don't seem to have taken the British to heart in the same way as Walmart has its American consumers. I've included a link later in the book as a starting point as to where the supermarkets appear to stand (no doubt information will change over time), so don't throw any blame my way if Security kicks you out!

Now, although we could imagine America being RV-friendly, Steve and I wondered how people would fare on the narrower British roads. Perish the thought of trying to navigate an RV down one of our Cornish country lanes. However, on reflection, they don't seem that different from coaches, and *they* usually manage to follow bus routes along narrow lanes with no problem – so why not an RV? Still, I wouldn't fancy it myself, and the sheer price of an RV would put me off – I think I'd rather buy a smaller motorhome and stay in a luxury hotel now and then instead.

As well as selling RVs, the Itchy Feet outlet we visited in Cornwall also rented out pitches and had a neighbouring golf course, plus swimming, sauna and fitness facilities for hire. So, even if you'd originally intended to take your rig out for a test-drive to see if it got stuck up a country lane or not, you'd probably end up getting distracted by all the on-site activities instead.

We also realised later that we hadn't seen any Romahomes while we were at the show. These are like small vans with a bed setup and mini kitchen in the back. Many have pop-up tops, making them versatile and economical. Their size makes them easy to drive into municipal car parks (which often have height restrictions). And, if you're catching a ferry to the continent, a lower head height can mean a cheaper ticket. Fuel economy would keep down the price of an overseas touring holiday too. The beds also look easy to set up in these, although from internet pictures, I couldn't see much cupboard space to speak of. In that respect, they might be fine for weekend getaways, but didn't seem so good for longer spells away.

As we drove back to my sister's, I felt that even just a half day spent looking round the show had been well worth the money. We got to check out so many makes of 'van – new and old – and got a better idea of the layouts, designs and internal space, which was invaluable. It's even somewhere you can take the kids, and you could easily make a day of it and take a picnic. But ladies, just remember that your husband is also likely to turn into a big kid when faced with all those campers!

The next day was warm and sunny with inviting blue skies and fluffy white clouds – welcome reminders that summer hadn't quite let go yet. And, with such lovely weather, we decided upon an easy day, wandering about the Sunday car boot sale at Cheddar.

When you mention 'Cheddar', most people will think straight away of a well-known, tasty cheese brand. So it's fair to forewarn eager, cheese-loving readers that the Cheddar car boot isn't a sales venue for regional cheeses, but a general car boot sale.

Now, along similar linguistic lines, I'd better clarify things for any non-Brits reading this who have never heard of car boots or car boot sales. For starters, 'car boot' might translate as 'trunk' in some versions of English. Once that's clear, one may still be left wondering: why would anyone want to sell (or buy!) a car boot? Well, people aren't *selling* car boots, they're selling stuff *from* their car boots. (Or that's the theory. And, to confuse the issue even more, the wares usually get transferred onto a table, thus taking the actual car boot out of the equation.) The same concept applies to our 'table top sales'. There are lots of those about, too, and again, no-one is selling the tops off tables. They are putting their stuff onto a table top and selling it. It's all perfectly clear now, isn't it? Just take a breath before you read on...

Cheddar car boot was obviously very popular. Even with an entry fee of only £1 per car, someone had to be making a killing, I thought, as I got out of the car and scanned the car park. There were vehicles as far as the eye could see.

We ambled up the first aisle, our eyes latching onto the multitudes of remaining bargains. You barely knew where to look first. Surprisingly, at the end of the aisle, the view opened out to reveal an idyllic lake vista framed by gently-swaying grasses and trees. The water rippled calmly as a breeze brushed over its surface. It struck me then that, all the while our eyes had been darting about, perusing the car boot goodies, our minds reeling from the choices on offer, Mother Nature's perfect tranquillity had been there in the background all along, patiently waiting for someone to notice and appreciate it. The wind whispered her gentle song: that stillness is always available if we just let go of our constant need to 'do' and strive for a while.

Then, before long, we were back in the fray for another few aisles, the moments of stillness overwritten by thoughts of amassing goodies; and we finally bought a few books and a little bike for my nephew's birthday. After a snack in the car boot canteen, I waited outside while the others had a quick, last look around at the remaining stalls.

The end of the car boot saw oddments of rubbish blowing about the ground – supermarket carrier bags, bits of paper, an empty crisps packet, a squashed Styrofoam cup... They were like wisps of spinifex in a Wild West movie, the sort that tumble across the dusty road before the cowboys have their showdown. The stillness before the fight.

Eventually, everyone's shopping bug was purged and we all piled into the car, along with my nephew's bike, heading off to my sister's house for dinner.

Although we'd planned to leave mid to late morning the next day, the lazy Monday vibe had set in and we ended up drinking copious amounts of tea and chatting with my sister before tidying away the bed. A good 'van clean-up made us feel we were at last organised again. Even if belongings have a designated home in the 'van, constant use means they're always out on ledges or counters and it can quickly start to look messy in a small space.

The weather was a fickle partner. While yesterday had been warm and inviting, promising good things to come, Monday quickly became overcast with intermittent speckles of rain. Within twenty-four hours, warm summer had turned to cold autumn. We saw my little nephew off to his new nursery school before having a lunchtime snack and fired up the 'van to make our way to the next destination: Avebury in Wiltshire.

The trip from south Bristol shouldn't have taken that long, but since we got into the wrong lane (not for the first time) and were now heading for Bath town centre in rush hour, the time it took us to finally arrive at Avebury was out of all proportion, and the Tourist Information Centre was closed by the time we arrived. So we drove to our site, down a road thickly lined with trees. Kingstone's Farm at

Cadley was a CL on a working farm. On the edge of Savernake Forest, all was quiet and still – a welcome relief from the city and traffic jams of the afternoon.

Since we had no electricity for lighting, we set up our bed early. It was at times like these, when we were tired and the evenings drew in fast, that we wished we had a rock-and-roll or sliding bed frame, instead of our 'jigsaw' setup.

It was a slow start to the week: if we thought Monday was a lazy day, Tuesday was no better. There were other caravans and motorhomes in storage nearby on our site, and with the weather being so sluggish and damp, we felt like we were on the hallowed grounds of a motorhome graveyard. It was so quiet, we could've been in the Twilight Zone or a land where time had stopped. But after 'dawdling' about on site, we finally left Cadley the next day and headed for the town of Marlborough, only to dawdle some more, ducking into various shops to dodge the rain. One thing was certain: I was glad we weren't camping in a tent in this weather. Staying in a campervan was wet enough!

We managed to fit in a whistle-stop tour of the manor garden at Avebury and museum (named after Alexander Keiller, the archaeologist who worked the site) before heading off to our next site, another CL not far away near Calne at Cherhill. A sign advertising food at the Black Horse Inn coaxed us to stop off for fish and chips, which we polished off before bedding down.

Pulling back the curtain during the night, I could see the Pleiades constellation shimmering up above and the half moon, like a silvery light shining through a rent in the black velvet fabric of the night sky. Everything was still and peaceful.

By Wednesday, our dawdling days were over and we got up in decent time to take a quick look at the Cherhill White Horse down the road. According to the tourist blurb, this was cut into the hillside under the directions of a Dr Alsop of Calne, given by megaphone from the main road; and the centre of the horse's eye (4ft across) used to be filled with upturned bottles which would sparkle in the sunlight. The term 'leucipottomy' was coined to describe the cutting of such White Horses on hillsides, and it probably comes in quite handy here, given that Wiltshire is such a White Horse-abundant area.

The previous evening, we had joined the National Trust; and now that we were members, we could return to the car park at Avebury and park for free (as opposed to pay the £5 charged to mere mortals). We'd timed things right: a tour of the Avebury stone circle was due to start shortly, so we had time for a snack at the National Trust café. There were no meat sandwiches, so I was guessing it was a vegetarian café (pretty rare), and we ate the most delicious cake for afters – a sumptuous lemon and almond delight.

Our volunteer tour guide, Avril, gave us a great introduction to Avebury's large Neolithic stone circle, using visual aids as we went. Without these, there's no way I would've got my head round the site. Firstly, because of the sheer scale of it (bigger than the village!) and secondly, because many of the stones have been moved. Even the smallest stone circle here is larger than the more famous Stonehenge on Salisbury Plain; and, just as with Stonehenge, speculation continues as to its true origins and meaning. Yet, for now, it all remains a mystery.

The tour over, we visited the local shop to replenish our bread and milk supplies. The store was run by volunteers and promoted local products, like delicious cake, locally-brewed ale and photo cards. The shop assistant was most bubbly and, when asked by a customer whether they had any national newspapers, she replied that they didn't stock them because they were too depressing. *What a great philosophy*, I thought. Just how many shops would cease to stock papers for that reason? Amazing!

We ambled back to our camper loaded up with locally-produced goodies and had a snack, washed down with a hot brew whilst thinking about how to best use our remaining time in Avebury. We soon fired up our mini rig and headed off briefly to nearby sites: The Sanctuary, and West Kennet Long Barrow near Silbury Hill.

The Sanctuary was one of those sites where you wonder if the archaeologists are having a bit of a joke with the public, since there aren't any actual original stones here. According to the information board, once upon a time, there had been stones and wooden posts on this site which formed a circular pattern. Now, each had been marked out by way of red and blue painted blocks.

West Kennet Long Barrow, supposedly one of the longest burial mounds in the world, is a short walk from the better-known, pudding bowl-shaped Silbury Hill (we didn't visit the latter: given the fence-line, it didn't look accessible).

As we reached the Barrow, I saw a guided group outside and followed not long behind as they made their way in. Inside were small chambers, and the tour leader started doing a bit of drumming, the theory being that the chambers had certain acoustic properties (ie vibrations) used for healing. Sounds far-fetched, but if sonic weapons exist, capable of destruction, then is it so far a leap to think sound can be used to do the opposite, and heal?

Feeling strangely stirred up after the drumming, I popped outside for a bit of fresh air. The rest of the group finally came out and we ended up walking back down the hill to the road (Steve had already wandered off to the 'van by this time). It turned out that the tourists were from my birthplace (Australia) and were over this neck of the woods to do a bit of travelling and check out their family history. But, despite my interesting encounter, it was a relief to get out of the wind and into the 'van, which had warmed up via passive solar heat. It was just as if someone had plugged in a radiator!

Large logs and hay rolls lined our way into our next site at Horse Lane Farm at Rowde near Devizes. By now, we were glad to have electric hookup so we could cool the contents of our fridge. Had we known before we set off that we'd be without a cool space for a while, we would've left the vegetables behind in our fridge at home (where they'd rot more slowly), buying what we needed as we went. One nifty trick we used to save our vehicle's resources (gas or 12 volt) was to put cool-blocks in the freezer compartment to ice up overnight when we had mains hookup, then put them in the fridge section during the day when off-site.

Although you can do without electricity, going without for a few days really makes you appreciate the amenities we all take for granted each day. If we hadn't had gas to cook on, though, we probably would've had to 'do a Ray Mears' and build a fire or something – although I'm not sure the site owners would have gone along with that, somehow.

As we hadn't had electric hookup for some days, it dawned on us how easy it could be to drive off without unplugging the electric cable from the mains outlet. I imagined a scenario in which the cable had accidentally been left connected to the 'van, ripping a trail of underground cabling as we drove away. Although it probably wouldn't happen that way in reality (and I don't care to put it to the test), I'm sure *some* damage would be done – either to the 'van or the mains connector. In any case, as with the aforementioned fire-making scenario, it's better all round if you just don't do it in the first place. Another safety check that should be carried out, of course, is switching off the gas valve. However, we've occasionally forgotten to do so, with no apparent harm done. And I'm not really sure how great the danger is if you leave it turned on.

We left the site and headed into Devizes. I'd heard it was a nice little town, so we thought we'd peruse it, and bought a one-hour parking ticket at the beloved Pay and Display machine. We stumbled (not quite literally) on a curious little pyramid monument, with a plaque explaining that the town's name came from the Latin term 'ad divisas', or 'at the boundary', since it stands at the meeting point of three manor boundaries.

At first glance, you could walk through the town in a few easy steps. Would we really need a whole hour's worth of ticket? I wondered. But then we turned a corner and it was suddenly apparent that there was more to the town than met the eye. What looked like a main shopping street had a fantastic busker in it. Now, I've pitied shop staff in the past who have had to listen to torturously-bad street entertainers, but I couldn't help thinking that this chap should've been Council-funded, since his soothing tones surely must have lulled shoppers into a purse-string-loosening, alpha state of mind.

A quaint side-alley opened out into what was obviously the town square, since a decent-sized market was bustling away, with a variety of clothes, fish and cheese stalls, along with the usual purveyors of fruit and veg who are only ever out-done by meat-stall owners for their vocal acumen and sales patter.

By the time we'd had what seemed like a quick look around the market, we were wishing we'd bought a two-hour parking ticket, just so that we didn't have to hurry back to the 'van.

In any case, we got back right on the dot and set off for our next destination, stopping at the lesser-known Woodhenge for lunch before 'going for gold' with a visit to the infamous Stonehenge. Like The Sanctuary, Woodhenge is another of those sites where what was originally (allegedly) there is now mapped out with posts. In this case, concrete posts marked out six concentric circles, which were probably timber posts supporting a circular Neolithic building.

***

We drove to Stonehenge. It was now mid-afternoon in the middle of September, when I would've guessed it to be quiet, yet there was a steady river of people flowing round it. How busy must it have been in July and August, the main British holiday season? The last time I'd been here was about twenty years ago. Had I just come at a quiet time of year back then, or was my memory of my previous visit failing me? In any case, the entry fees would no doubt help to swell the region's coffers.

Although Stonehenge is looked after by the English Heritage, they have a reciprocal agreement of some kind with the National Trust, so we got in for free. The audio tour is available in ten languages. We only needed one. We donned our earphones and got the scoop on this World Heritage Site which has been aged at around five thousand years old, and is aligned with the rising and setting of the sun at the solstices.

Taking snaps at certain points wasn't easy, due to the other pesky tourist bods – and getting a picture without anyone else in it was even harder. You'd just have to Photoshop them out later. A rope cordoned off the stones from grubby tourist hands and feet – apparently, only those hands and feet with special permission can get close to them!

The whole process of tourist through-put was professionally done; and if you felt you hadn't spent enough already on transport costs and entry fees, there was always the usual selection of 'must have' gifts to relieve you of your hard-earned in the shop on the way out. Fancy a Stonehenge glitter snowglobe (could double up as a handy paperweight) or mini model of the monument (doubles up as a tongue-twister)?

We left Stonehenge and headed for our next site at Orcheston. I'd printed off a map from the internet before leaving home, but the circle pinpointing the site was in the wrong place. I'd noticed this happening before with rural sites – probably because the postcode covers a wide area. In the end, we just aimed ourselves in the general direction, winding through village lanes with houses sporting unusual patterned flint stonework, before signs appeared, guiding us to the Stonehenge Touring Park site.

For a change, we weren't staying on a Caravan Club site. Surprisingly, there were very few campsites near Stonehenge – certainly, I found nothing within a short walking distance, as I had hoped. In fact, our site was so popular at solstice times, that the owner said they were booked up a year in advance!

Our pitch must have been one of the loveliest on the site, I remarked, as we drove into our spot. Perched beneath the shade of a tree, we parked to face fields – one containing two horses, the other two cows. Over a welcome cuppa, we watched a cow and bull affectionately licking each others' coats whilst lazily swishing their tails in the early evening sun.

A couple of lads ran up to the fence to pat the horse and left just as quickly. It was then that I spotted plums on the edge of the next pitch, which was currently empty. I plucked a few ripe ones and got Steve to pick the ones I couldn't reach. I was amazed at how sweet they were – especially as they can sometimes be a bit sour.

It wasn't the first time we'd spotted fruit on our journey which would otherwise have gone to waste. Apple trees seemed to be everywhere in Wiltshire – some looked ripe, whilst other fruits were still developing. Ironic, I thought, how there are all these free, unsprayed apples going to waste when everyone goes out and pays a premium to buy them from a supermarket – and ones that are often flown in from abroad, at that!

As I stuck my head out the door the next morning, nothing and no-one stirred. I looked around and noticed that the campers a couple of pitches down had left early, yet we hadn't heard them dismantling their tent. I breathed in a lungful of fresh air and watched a robin tugging at whatever was emerging from the pitch's bald-spot, before going back inside to make a cuppa. We opened our front curtains to a picture window of horses nuzzling together and cows munching on grass. Then, as we drank, a kestrel surprisingly flew down and perched on the fence post in the field.

We'd booked this site for two nights, which meant we could, if we wanted, just chill out today. Tomorrow was Saturday and we'd be going home anyway. Certainly, watching the animals in the fields made you feel like there was no rush to do anything. But after a lazy sit-in, it was too hard to resist getting out in the fair weather, and we headed to Old Sarum, not that far away.

This large Iron Age hill fort, run by English Heritage, encircles the ruins of a castle and royal palace. You even get to see the regal toilet pit which some poor servant had to clean out. I expect things were so bad in those days that he probably boasted about the job!

From the ramparts, there was a panoramic vista of the surrounding area, with Salisbury cathedral on one side, and the countryside and remains of a cathedral (within the boundaries of Old Sarum) on the other. Several planes flew overhead as we wandered round; no doubt the aerial photos of the site used for tourism purposes were taken by someone hiring a plane from the local airfield.

After negotiating the roadworks and streets of nearby Amesbury to get petrol, we joined the Friday afternoon traffic jams on the main roads. We still couldn't get over how busy the area was. The traffic, it seemed, was like litmus, warning us that the pH value of our campsite was about to change; for Friday night on site was very different from our quiet Thursday evening. When we finally got back with an almighty *Phew!*, the site looked fully booked for the weekend, with a group of families tucked into one large corner, lighting a barbecue and celebrating someone's birthday (probably one of the kids' – but still a good excuse for a booze-up) until the eleven o'clock noise restriction kicked in.

Surprisingly, we were ready to head home before ten o'clock the next morning – which had to be a record for us, as we hadn't even rushed to pack. One of our site neighbours must have left around the same time, because we kept crossing paths with them on the roads. Either that, or there was some conspiracy going on here and we were being tailed.

Petrol prices dipped suddenly by several pence per litre as we crossed the border from Wiltshire into Devon, such that we wondered if the signs were wrong.

It was a glorious, sunny day with blue skies; and, as we hadn't seen enough motorhomes at the Shepton Mallet show the week before, we decided to pop into Martins of Exeter on the way back – a caravan and motorhome sales outlet that we'd always missed visiting for one reason or another whenever we passed that way.

Some motorhomes were in good nick on the site, whilst others were on the worn side. We had a look at a couple of caravans as well. For the price, it seemed you got a lot of space. If you only needed one vehicle in the household, a caravan might be more appropriate than a motorhome, as you don't have to traipse your living space about everywhere. Caravans can also serve as a spare room, eg for visitors to kip over in. You can also keep your holiday stuff in them, taking a break away at the drop of a hat. However, you do have to learn to manoeuvre them properly, which some people either don't like or can't get to grips with (although there are dedicated courses for this). They also aren't as stable in high winds, and their length means you can't stop off that easily at some places en route.

The drive back home sort of marked the end of an era for us. Our one-year experiment in having a campervan was over, although it looked like we'd be keeping the 'van for a while longer yet. Buying a bigger rig didn't appeal to us right now – particularly from the point of view of parking, manoeuvrability and fuel consumption, although I liked how roomy they were.

There is probably something inherently nomadic in a motorhomer's spirit that lies dormant until, one day, it's triggered by seeing the likes of a campervan. And, given my obviously itchy-footed disposition, it was nice to know that I could satisfy the wanderlust of my youth to some degree with our campervan whilst keeping my current lifestyle going.

All in all, it seems to me that the ideal motorhome would be like a Tardis: small on the outside and massive on the inside. Even though we'll still keep an eye out in case we spot something else we like, I think we'll stick with what we've got for the moment.

But if anyone invents a Tardis-like motorhome like this, do let us know…

EPILOGUE – The End of the Road?

Since the end of our first year's experiment in autumn 2010, we've continued to explore the world of campervanning, and we're continually amazed at how many things there are still to learn.

After a winter break, we began spring of 2011 with a trip to the Isle of Wight off the south coast, followed by several closer-to-home journeys in Cornwall and Devon. You can read about these 'mini adventures' (and enjoy a few photos) in our Campervan Capers blog. Also look out for *Campervan Capers 2* – a free, handy eBook adapted from the blog (links coming up later).

So far, we haven't taken the plunge and upgraded to a model with a quick-setup bed and shower unit. Still, it's on our 'wish list' and I'm sure something will crop up when we're ready for a new 'van.

My dream now is to do more travelling in Europe. This, of course, brings up the question of whether it is more cost effective to travel in the camper or to sell it and take a ferry or plane to the Continent and stay in a hotel or caravan. But, so far, we haven't felt it was time to let go of "Old Bessie", as Steve now calls the camper. And as I write this epilogue in early 2012, Steve and I are planning to take a trip to Belgium, stopping off to visit the caves of the Ardennes and looping back to catch the Tour of Flanders bicycle race (I did say he had ulterior motives when he got that bike rack fitted, didn't I?).

Overseas travel, it seems, is another area of exploration again, and we're eager to continue learning as we go and sharing our experiences. So why not check out our travel tales on the blog, where we also pass on tips we've picked up along the way. In addition, all our travel photos (whether from the stories in this book or the blog) can be found in one handy place on Flickr, including a map of our trips (link at end of book).

We might have reached the end of our first year's experiment in campervanning, but it certainly isn't the end of the road... Not yet, at least...

I haven't done a formal 'Acknowledgments' section in this book, so I'd like to fit in a thank you here to my partner, Steve... Thanks for your support, making our trips that much more fun, bouncing ideas around with me, giving me feedback, etc etc…(I could go on…)

Well, I hope you've enjoyed reading about our adventures – although the book doesn't quite end here, as there are still a few goodies you might like to read…

Stay tuned for…

30 Top Tips for the Novice
Considerations when Buying a Motorhome or Caravan
My infamous 'faux reviews' by pseudo-celebrities…
plus
Find out more about me and my other titles…

30 TOP TIPS for the Novice

Although Steve and I are learning all the time – and therefore, in many ways, still novices ourselves – I hope the tips we've picked up will be useful to readers, in particular, those just setting out in the world of campervanning.

This section covers some general basics and is followed by another section with more specific considerations when buying a 'van. These tips are not intended to be exhaustive and I do not claim to be any sort of authority on the subject. Later in the book, there are also links to websites which you may find useful.

PRACTICAL TIPS

1. **Check systems before going away** – eg leisure battery charged, fridge functioning, etc.
2. **Keep a set of levellers on board.** Not all sites are flat or have hard standing.
3. **Be mindful of your 'van size.** When new to motorhoming, it's easy to forget you're in a larger vehicle. Pay particular attention with height-restricted car parks, and low tree branches and hedgerows on narrow country lanes.
4. **Purchase an aqua-roll** if you use a lot of water. These roll-along water containers are much easier to manoeuvre than portable ones.
5. **Memory foam** can make for a more comfy night's sleep, even in a more expensive motorhome.
6. **An up-to-date map** (or GPS) is invaluable. Even so, follow directions in club directories in preference to your GPS or what seems like a short cut on the map. These may help you avoid trouble spots for motorhomes and caravans.
7. **Smaller, micro-fibre flannels or towels** take up less space than larger standard towels and can be quickly washed and dried.
8. **Take spare torches** to use on site at night, plus other lighting if you're on a site without electricity.

9. **Invest in clothing** for your trip that's light and fast-drying. It'll store more easily, and because it dries so quickly after washing, the 'van will feel less like a laundry room.
10. **A small, collapsible drier** is useful not only for drying clothes but also for airing duvets and blankets – great for 'van freshening on longer trips.
11. **Take a bicycle (pedal or rechargeable electric) or use local bus services** if you have a larger motorhome – save on parking fees and avoid problems finding suitable parking in town.
12. **Consider the advantages and disadvantages of awnings**. Plus side: they offer shelter, an extra room, and are useful for wet gear. Down side: they take time and effort to put up and down, and you should (ideally) air them out or clean them ASAP thereafter. Sites may charge for awnings.
13. **If you have a smaller vehicle or want to simplify** your packing, ask if you *need* or *want* items. Do you really need many entertainments? Or will they detract from your holiday explorations?
14. **Research cheaper fuel stops** on the internet to save money.
15. **Budget for inevitable parking fees** while you're away and keep plenty of change handy. Free parking may be available, but you might have to search for it.
16. **Check gas bottle levels** before going away. If low, buy a spare or research stockists to visit en route.
17. **If buying a larger caravan or motorhome**, ensure you're happy and confident driving it, especially down narrower lanes. Special courses exist to learn how to manoeuvre them correctly & safely.
18. **Shop around for insurance and breakdown cover.** If you're a motorhome club member, get a quote from their affiliates. How do they compare with other quotes?

GETTING THE MOST out of your HOLIDAY CHOICES

19. **Think differently about your holidays** now that you have a motorhome. Why not have more, shorter breaks away instead of the usual one or two longer holidays a year?
20. **Make a list of your interests and places** you'd really like to visit. Refer to your list often and use it to guide your holiday choices.

21. **For a quieter or cheaper holiday**, go away in low/mid season. High season will be more expensive and sites will be busier.
22. **Out of season, check opening times** before you go if you're intent upon visiting a certain tourist destination. Some open for only a few days a week. Others change routine or close altogether.
23. **Use the internet to compare sites**, get a feel for them, and to match your needs to the site details. If you definitely want to stay on a site at a given time, verify availability and confirm prices beforehand.
24. **Out of high season,** you may not need to pre-book a site. Great news if you like to travel where the wind takes you. Still, a word of warning: certain events held in the otherwise low season might mean accommodation is fully booked.
25. **If you want a less bustling holiday**, there are often sites near the hotspots which are quieter, yet which still leave you within easy reach of the tourist sights.
26. **Membership of an organisation** – eg National Trust or English Heritage – is handy, even if only for a year. Get maximum benefit by basing visits around their destinations – there's often free parking, too.
27. **Consider joining a club** for caravan or motorhome owners. Regular in-house magazines and discounts at their designated sites are just some of the benefits membership can bring.

TIPS for WINTER

28. **Tips for avoiding mustiness in your 'van**: air the 'van when weather permits; remove seat blocks, bedding and blankets, placing them indoors near a radiator; use a dehumidifier or warm-air fan; place tubs of salt inside to absorb moisture.
29. **Keep your eye out for rust problems**. Fix ASAP (especially as the 'van gets older) to keep rust manageable, save you money in the long run, and keep the 'van desirable for when you come to sell it.
30. **Drain the on-board water tank over winter** (unless it's an enclosed, insulated type). If drinking water from the tank when refilled, people are advised to use sanitising tablets to keep the water free of bacteria.

CONSIDERATIONS WHEN BUYING
A Motorhome or Caravan

BEFORE PURCHASE:

Check the 'van's bed setup. Know the advantages and disadvantages of each sort and choose according to your needs. Try putting the bed together, ensuring you're happy with it, and that all pieces are present and correct.

Consider the 'van's uses. Do you want a motorhome solely for holidays or to double as a work vehicle? How will this affect your choice of size, fuel economy and so on?

Where and when do you plan to holiday? An older 'van will usually be less well insulated than a more modern one. Something to consider if holidaying in colder climes or at colder times of year.

Motorhome shows are a great way to check out a wide variety of campers and caravans, as well as accessories.

Think through your needs carefully before putting down a deposit. A few useful questions are as follows:

Is it time for you to buy a motorhome yet?
Can you realistically afford one?
If so, *what* can you comfortably afford?
What do you want in a motorhome?
What do you envisage using it for?
Do you just want a weekender 'van or will you be going away for longer periods?
How much space do you personally need?
Will you be happy with a smaller 'van or do you need more room to manoeuvre?
Have you got kids – and how will they fit in?
What is the fuel consumption like?

Does your health or age require an easy-setup bed?
Do I want to get a basic check done on the 'van, or am I happy to risk a purchase?

Considerations when thinking of upgrading to another 'van:
What am I hoping to obtain in the process?
Do I really need a new one, or can I make changes to the 'van I already have?
What am I willing to compromise on, and what not?
What would I be considering upgrading to, and can I afford it?
List the negatives about your current 'van and turn them around to find out what you're seeking in a new 'van.

Romahomes – some advantages and disadvantages: On the plus side, they have good fuel economy, are versatile (some with pop-up tops) and, at the size of a small 'van, would be cheaper to run round the country or Europe. Having said that, check you're happy with the more limited storage space if going away on longer trips.

Caravans – some advantages and disadvantages: On the plus side, you don't have to traipse your living space about, and you can keep your holiday stuff in it whilst running your household vehicle around separately. On the down side, you need to ensure you can reverse them, they are less stable in high winds, and if you want to stop off en route, you need to ensure adequate parking space.

Having a motorhome or caravan is a work-in-progress. Buy a 'van, try it out for a while, and it'll reflect back to you what you'll need in your next 'van. But remember: you *may* lose money by buying without thinking things through.

AFTER PURCHASE:

Habitation checks. Done by a qualified specialist, these will give you feedback on the condition of your 'van in terms of its structure, fixtures and fittings.

Mechanical checks. If you didn't get your 'van checked before purchase, why not get a 'health check' from a garage afterwards. This will point out any work that needs doing and you can iron out problems before the MOT comes up.

Get to know your 'van, whether it's new or old. Check out the manual (if you have one) as well as the nooks and crannies. Make sure everything you need for a trip away is present and correct, replacing anything that's missing, broken or faulty.

Fitting a bicycle rack may be an added cost but is well worth it if you or your family cycle regularly.

Check out local outlets that sell motorhome products or do campervan-specific repairs. If you know others with a motorhome in your area, ask for advice. It's amazing what can be available in your local area that you never heard about before.

USEFUL WEBLINKS for each Chapter

The following links pertain to each chapter and give relevant site details, tourist information and other references. We have found many of the links useful along our own journey, although I do not endorse one site, company or website over another, putting the onus on the reader to discern the information provided and to decide what is most useful and relevant for them.

I have listed below only non-Caravan Club campsites, so as to avoid repeating links for the Caravan Club which we stayed in frequently. You can find out more about the Club's main sites and 'CL' sites at www.caravanclub.co.uk (you must be a member to stay on the latter).

Photos from our travels can be found on Flickr at www.flickr.com/photos/alannah_foley/sets, along with a map showing an overview of trips.

Links were correct at completion of the book's manuscript, so I apologise if any have since become defunct. These will be checked and updated as necessary in subsequent editions of the book.

1 MAIDEN VOYAGE

SITE LINKS
- Twelve Oaks Farm Caravan Park, Teigngrace, nr Newton Abbot, Devon
  www.twelveoaksfarm.co.uk

TOURIST LINKS
- Dartmoor National Park
  www.dartmoor-npa.gov.uk
- Stover Country Park (Nature Reserve), nr Newton Abbot, Devon
  www.devon.gov.uk/stover_country_park

OTHER LINKS
- Outdoor Experience, Teingrace, nr Newton Abbot, Devon
  www.outdoorexperience.co.uk

2 THE UNDISCOVERED DOORSTEP

SITE LINKS
- Roselands Park, nr St Just, Cornwall
  www.roselands.co.uk

TOURIST LINKS
- Chysauster Ancient Village (north of Penzance, Cornwall) – English Heritage
  www.english-heritage.org.uk/chysauster
- Geevor Tin Mine, nr Pendeen, Cornwall
  www.geevor.com
- Cornwall
  www.visitcornwall.com

OTHER LINKS
- Re: overnight roadside parking
  www.go4awalk.com/ask/campervanparking.php

3 STRETCHING OUR WHEELS

SITE LINKS
- The Old Oaks Farm site, Glastonbury
  www.theoldoaks.co.uk

TOURIST LINKS
- Glastonbury Tor – National Trust site
  www.nationaltrust.org.uk/glastonbury-tor
- Glastonbury Tor – general/esoteric site
  www.glastonburytor.org.uk
- Wookey Hole Caves, Somerset
  www.wookey.co.uk

4 THE WELSH LEEK CONSPIRACY

SITE LINKS
- Three Cliffs Bay Holiday Park, Gower Peninsula, Wales
  www.threecliffsbay.com

- Dan-yr-Ogof Campsite – see link below

TOURIST LINKS
- The Mumbles, Gower Peninsula, Wales
  www.mumbles.co.uk
- Gower Wildflower and Local Produce Centre, Gower Peninsula, Wales… At last try, the original web address I had for them was defunct: www.gowerwildflowers.co.uk.
- Aberdulais Falls, Vale of Neath, Wales – National Trust
  www.nationaltrust.org.uk/aberdulais-tinworks-and-waterfall
- Dan-yr-Ogof Caves, Powys, Wales (incl. campsite)
  www.showcaves.co.uk
- Brecon Beacons, Wales
  www.visitbreconbeacons.com
- Westonbirt National Arboretum, Gloucestershire
  www.westonbirtarboretum.com

OTHER LINKS
- Vicarious Books – overseas motorhoming (Aires/France Passion, etc)
  http://vicariousbooks.co.uk
- Motorhome Parking – Law re: overnight roadside parking
  www.motorhomeparking.co.uk/roads.htm
- Motorhome Parking – website detailing friendly and unfriendly parking. The following is the most comprehensive site I found. Includes links all over Great Britain for detailed info from Councils, and info on parking at motorway services, supermarkets, etc.:
  www.motorhomeparking.co.uk

5 DAMP SQUIBS & SNOWY ROOFTOPS
- 12 Volt Shop
  (Now appears to operate as an online business – based in St Austell, Cornwall)
  www.the12voltshop.co.uk

6 OUT OF HIBERNATION

- The Caravan Club
  www.caravanclub.co.uk
- The Camping and Caravanning Club
  www.campingandcaravanningclub.co.uk

7 DAWDLING ROUND DORSET

TOURIST LINKS

- Durdle Door
  www.durdledoor.org.uk
- Jurassic Coast World Heritage Site
  www.jurassiccoast.com
- Portland Bill Lighthouse
  www.trinityhouse.co.uk/lighthouses/lighthouse_list/portland_bill.html
- Weymouth Tourist Information
  www.visitweymouth.co.uk

OTHER

- AA guide we used: 365 Pub Walks and Cycle Rides in Britain – ISBN 978-0-7495-6372-1

8 PEAK EXPERIENCES

TOURIST LINKS for Derbyshire

- Manifold Valley – Walking and Cycling Map (printable leaflet)
  www.simonholtmarketing.com/PDFs/Manifold%20Valley%20Leaflet2.pdf
- Thor's Cave and Manifold Valley Walk
  www.snapthepeaks.co.uk/Walks/Thors/thors.htm
- Tissington Trail
  www.peakdistrictinformation.com/visits/tisstrail.php
- Peak District
  www.visitpeakdistrict.com
- Poole's Cavern, Buxton
  www.poolescavern.co.uk

- Speedwell Cavern, Castleton, Hope Valley
  www.speedwellcavern.co.uk
- Peak Cavern, Castleton, Hope Valley
  www.devilsarse.com
- Treak Cliff Cavern, Castleton, Hope Valley
  www.bluejohnstone.com
- Blue John Cavern, Castleton, Hope Valley
  www.bluejohn-cavern.co.uk
- The Heights of Abraham, Matlock Bath
  www.heightsofabraham.com
- Cascades Gardens, Bonsall, Nr Matlock
  www.derbyshiregarden.com

OTHER LINKS

- Visit Underground (Natural Caves and Underground Attractions in Britain and Ireland)
  www.visitunderground.com
- Bakewell Puddings (not tarts!)
  www.peakdistrict-nationalpark.com/bakewell-pudding.aspx

OTHER

- AA guide we used: 365 Pub Walks and Cycle Rides in Britain – ISBN 978-0-7495-6372-1

9 JOURNEY TO THE PAST

TOURIST LINKS

- Cannock Chase, Staffordshire
  www.visitcannockchase.co.uk
- Fradley Junction, Staffordshire
  www.ldb.co.uk/lichfield/fradley.htm
- Lichfield, Staffordshire
  www.visitlichfield.co.uk
- Burnham-on-Sea
  www.burnham-on-sea.com/tourism.shtml

OTHER LINKS

- Caravan Club courses for Caravan/Motorhome Manoeuvring

www.caravanclub.co.uk/expert-advice/
  getting-started/training-courses
- Camping and Caravanning Club courses for
  Caravan/Motorhome Manoeuvring
  www.campingandcaravanningclub.co.uk/
  helpandadvice/courses/manoeuvringcourses
- Tips: "Keep bugs from sticking to the front of your vehicle"
  www.rvquicktips.com/2012/02/
  remove-those-nasty-bugs-after-long.html

10 STAR-STRUCK

TOURIST LINKS
- Burgh Island Hotel, near Bigbury-on-Sea, Devon
  www.burghisland.com
- Burgh Island and surrounds – AA suggested walk
  www.theaa.com/walks/burgh-island-paradise-420286
- Bigbury-on-Sea, Devon
  www.bigburyonsea.co.uk
- Hope Cove, Devon
  www.devon-online.com/towns/salcombe/hopecove.html
- Winking Prawn Café, North Sands, Devon
  http://winkingprawn.co.uk
- Salcombe, Devon
  www.salcombeinformation.co.uk

OTHER LINKS
- CAT (Centre for Alternative Technology),
  Machynlleth, Powys, Wales
  www.cat.org.uk
- Awning Care Tips
  www.rvtravel.com/publish/article_445.shtml

11 THE MAGIC OF CORNWALL

SITE LINKS
- Magic Cove Touring Park, Mawgan Porth, nr Newquay, Cornwall
  www.magiccove.co.uk

TOURIST LINKS
- Newquay, Cornwall
  www.visitnewquay.org

12 DIPPING INTO DEVON

TOURIST LINKS
- Ayrmer Cove, near Ringmore, Devon – National Trust
  www.nationaltrust.org.uk/visit/local-to-you/
  south-west/view-page/item539258
- AA suggested walk – via Ayrmer Cove and Bigbury/Burgh Island, Devon
  www.theaa.com/walks/burgh-island-paradise-420286
- Plymbridge Woods, nr Plympton, Devon – National Trust
  www.nationaltrust.org.uk/visit/local-to-you/
  south-west/view-page/item591855

13 MODERN WHEELS & ANCIENT STONES

SITE LINKS
- Stonehenge Touring Park, Orcheston, Salisbury, Wiltshire
  http://stonehengetouringpark.com

TOURIST LINKS
NB: Since our visit to Avebury, I've discovered that some sites in the area are owned by the National Trust whilst being managed by English Heritage and vice versa; and some are privately owned and managed by either of these organisations. It seems a little different for each site, so I've listed links below for you to check current information before visiting.
- Avebury
  www.english-heritage.org.uk/daysout/properties/avebury
  www.nationaltrust.org.uk/avebury
- Alexander Keiller Museum, Avebury
  www.english-heritage.org.uk/daysout/properties/
  avebury-alexander-keiller-museum
  www.nationaltrust.org.uk/things-to-see-and-do/
  page-2/item257410

- The Sanctuary, Avebury
  www.english-heritage.org.uk/daysout/properties/the-sanctuary
- West Kennet Long Barrow, Avebury
  www.english-heritage.org.uk/daysout/properties/west-kennet-long-barrow
- Silbury Hill, Avebury
  www.english-heritage.org.uk/daysout/properties/silbury-hill
- Woodhenge, Salisbury
  www.english-heritage.org.uk/woodhenge
- Stonehenge, Salisbury Plain
  (Also free entry for National Trust members)
  www.english-heritage.org.uk/stonehenge
- Old Sarum, Salisbury
  www.english-heritage.org.uk/oldsarum

OTHER LINKS

- Motorhome and US RV Show
  Not sure of our original information source about the Shepton Mallet show we attended, but there is a list of shows at this address:
  www.ukmotorhomes.net/motorhome-shows.shtml
- Itchy Feet (RVs and Motorhomes)
  I believe the situation has changed on site since we visited… The sales side of the business now appears to be dealt with via:
  http://itchyfeetmotorhomes.com
  However, the outlet we visited still seems to have motorhome pitches available. Visit the following link for current info if interested:
  www.carvynick.co.uk/touring-park
- RV Travel
  A very useful American site run by RVers – they have a free newsletter, lots of info and links on RVing, plus an RV bookstore
  http://rvtravel.com
- Walmart Atlas (which Walmarts permit free overnight stay)
  http://rvbookstore.com/shop/detail.aspx?p=1280&m=2
- RV Boondocking News
  Article re: shooting in Walmart parking lot:
  "Could this foretell the end of overnighting at Walmart?"

www.rvboondockingnews.com/2010/08/could-this-be-end-of-overnighting-at.html
- UK Supermarkets – Re: Overnight Parking www.motorhomeparking.co.uk/stores.htm
- Martins of Exeter (caravan and motorhome sales) – Off Junct 30 of the M5 www.martinsofexeter.co.uk

FAUX REVIEWS by Pseudo-Celebrities for Campervan Capers

"Forget Formula One! It isn't a patch on driving one of these turbo-charged babies. And I never would have tried one out if it weren't for reading this little book. Only downside is, site owners aren't keen on you cutting up their lawns and using their sites as a racetrack."
Nigel Mannsul

"Since buying a motorhome myself, I've realised the campervan world isn't just a bunch of down-and-out gypsy dossers. It's such a great alternative solution to the housing shortage that it should be encouraged. Anyone thinking of getting a 'van should definitely read *Campervan Capers*."
UK Prime Minister

"I heartily encourage a campervanning lifestyle! Getting out onto the open road, it's amazing just how much road-kill you can pick up... And, with a gas hob on board, I can fry up what I find on the spot."
Huw Fern-Leigh-Wit-In-Stall

"Who wants to be lumbered with a mortgage when you can doss around in one of these little beauties? Unfortunately, one already has one's own home and a handful of social engagements one must attend. But reading *Campervan Capers* certainly gave me a taste of life as one of the peasants."
Bonnie Prince Charlie

"*Campervan Capers* – great for anyone infected by the travelling bug... Err... Can I plug my own books now?"
Billy Brisun

"If you love campervanning, why not stay on one of my award-winning sites. They're all over the place. But I won't be there. I'll be too busy trimming my beard."
David Belle-Ami

"I go out in my camper to study insects. It's amazing how many different species you can collect on your windscreen as you drive full pelt along the motorway."
David Atinburrer

"After reading *Campervan Capers*, I saw the light and had a word with the 'Beeb'. Now they're up for a new series, with me circling the globe in a motorhome."
Michael Pailing

"I used to have an RV back in the great US of A. But then I came to this tiny little island called Britain and read *Campervan Capers*. My God! I was transformed – and bought one of those quaint little English campers instead. Downsizing sure has made me happy!"
Tom Crews

"Forget traipsing through the flippin' snow and ice at the poles. This book has converted me! You can snuggle down in a camper and just whack on the Propex if it gets a bit chilly. And adventures? I went to Margate and back on the weekend. At this rate, I'm sure I'll have another bestselling book out soon."
Randy Fines

N.B. – Disclaimer (To be referred to in cases of acute gullibility):
As denoted by 'faux' and 'pseudo', the above reviews are completely spurious in nature. Although they are loosely based on real-world characters, note that they do not reflect the opinions of any person, whether alive, dead or fictitious. Needless to say, no offense is intended upon the original characters.

ABOUT the Author

Born in Australia, Alannah Foley was raised in England and lived Down Under for five years in her twenties. Before returning to Old Blighty, she discovered long-lost family, stayed on a camel farm, worked on a City Farm project, and got bitten by every mozzie around.

Alannah enjoys drawing her observations & ideas together into whatever form seems appropriate – be it a book, short story, article, poem, or song. She is also an avid photographer and her images complement her writing in the Campervan Capers Blog.

The author has written *The Jacaranda Trail*, about her five-year stint Down Under; *Cycling Widows*; and *SHADES*, a collection of short fictional works. She has also written and illustrated a short story book for children called *Slowcoach Sid (NOT the Fastest Snail in the Garden!)*.

Alannah currently lives in Cornwall, England, with her cycling-obsessed partner.

Read on for more information…

CONNECT with the Author

Foley's Forum
www.foleysforum.co.uk
Alannah's main website
Go to Contact/Links page to get in touch
and for social networking links like Facebook

The Foley's Forum Blog
http://foleysforum.wordpress.com
Quick tour of Alannah's work and
latest news & offers

Campervan Capers Blog
http://campervancapers.wordpress.com
Check out Alannah's travel tales & photography

Alannah's Photos on Flickr
www.flickr.com/photos/alannah_foley/sets
Check out photos from the
Campervan Capers book & blog

Foley's Forum Videos – YouTube Channel
www.youtube.com/user/FoleysForumVideos/videos
A channel of short videos for Alannah's work

OTHER TITLES by Alannah Foley

For more information on the following titles,
visit the author's website at www.foleysforum.co.uk/books:

THE JACARANDA TRAIL
A Journey of Discovery Down Under

CYCLING WIDOWS
Lifting the Veil
on Living with an Obsessive Cyclist

SHADES
A Collection of Short Fictional Works

SLOWCOACH SID
(NOT the Fastest Snail in the Garden!)
A short story book for young children

~ FREE DOWNLOADS ~

As well as finding lots of free-to-read stories, articles and poetry on the author's website, you can download the following for free:

CAMPERVAN CAPERS 2
The Ongoing Adventures of a Campervanning Couple

THE WELSH LEEK CONSPIRACY
A light-hearted travel tale from *Campervan Capers*

UNDER AN AUSTRALIAN SKY
Reflections on Life Down Under

The INTREPID ADVENTURES of RALPH INGLETON
A Short Story from *SHADES*

Printed in Great Britain
by Amazon.co.uk, Ltd.,
Marston Gate.